THE
UNOFFICIAL
WEDNESDAY
COOKBOOK

✕

Recipes
Inspired by the
Deliciously Macabre
TV Show

 Iphigenia Jones

✕✕✕

ULYSSES PRESS

Published by:
ULYSSES PRESS
PO Box 3440
Berkeley, CA 94703
www.ulyssespress.com

ISBN: 978-1-64604-593-8
Library of Congress Control Number: 2023935649

Printed in the United States by Sheridan Books Minnesota
10 9 8 7 6 5 4 3 2 1

Contributing writer: Laura Laikko
Acquisitions editor: Casie Vogel
Managing editor: Claire Chun
Editor: Renee Rutledge
Proofreader: Barbara Schultz
Front cover design: David Hastings
Interior design: what!design @ whatweb.com
Layout: Winnie Liu
Illustrations and photos: shutterstock.com except photos on pages 22, 32, 52, 67, 84, 90, 98, 107, 114 © Michael Calcagno

FOR OUR OWN SPOOKY FAMILIES

CONTENTS

INTRODUCTION

Welcome, woeful readers, to our culinary journey through the wonderfully weird world of Wednesday.

In 1938, a cartoonist named Charles Addams introduced the world to the Addams family, a uniquely grim but *deeply* loving caricature of a nuclear family. Despite their violent hobbies and gothic sensibilities, the family cared for each other and their fearful neighbors. While other fictional families seemed to not even like one another, the Addamses worked together to create a happily unhappy household. Pop culture enthusiasts across the globe fell in love, and the freaky family has starred in dozens of spin-offs since: a beloved sitcom in the '60s, cult classic comedies in the '90s, animated films and, finally, a Netflix show. The family features a glamorously ghastly mother and father, a kooky uncle, a spooky butler, a loyal disembodied hand, and a strange son. But it's daughter Wednesday, with her double braids and murderous ways, who has captured the hearts and minds of a dreadfully large number of outcasts. The stoic little misanthrope finally took center stage in *Wednesday*, a show following a young adult Wednesday as she navigates the mysterious and magical halls of Nevermore Academy.

What is it about Wednesday, out of all the quirky family members, that draws us back again and again? There is something undeniable about the hilarious little goth girl, played brilliantly by every one of her actresses. Besides her quick wit and iconic fashion sensibilities, Wednesday speaks to the outcast in all of us. She not only understands the weirdest parts of us, she *welcomes* it! She demands that we reveal our innermost monsters, because that's the most interesting part of ourselves. While it's perhaps not morally acceptable in real life to dump piranhas in a swimming pool of bullies, it's deeply satisfying to watch straight-faced Jenna Ortega defend her little brother in the bloodiest way possible.

And Nevermore, with its curled gates and ominous stone facade, offers sanctuary for the monsters in all of us—whether we're gorgons with a secret or werewolves with an affinity for crochet. The school welcomes us and reaffirms the message that we're worthy of magic. No matter who you are or what you like, Wednesday is ready for you. Perhaps she'll judge you and threaten you with a guillotine, but that just means she's treating you like family.

I hope you'll enjoy our flavorful tribute to Wednesday, the Addamses, and Nevermore. Take a bite—it's not poison. At least, probably not this time.

WORD TO THE WOEFUL

In Chapter 4, Woe Your Whistle, note that many of the drinks are alcoholic beverages and intended only for legal adults. Adults have many more years of sorrows and are uniquely qualified for the taste of alcohol. Where it applies, we have included nonalcoholic versions of these drinks for younger souls who still have many terrifying years ahead of them.

WOE
D'OEUVRES

The boundaries which
divide Life from Death
are at best shadowy and
vague. Who shall say
where the one ends, and
where the other begins?

–Edgar Allan Poe,
"The Premature Burial"

BLOODY BREAKFAST SMOOTHIE

Early-morning classes can be difficult for creatures of the night, but vampire cliques find this smoothie provides a much-needed energy boost. If you'd like to try a similar beverage but have dietary restrictions that prevent you from drinking human blood, this beet-red substitute should work just fine.

Yield: 1 to 2 smoothies | Prep time: 10 to 12 minutes

1 medium beet, peeled and chopped

1 large banana, peeled and sliced

1 cup fresh spinach leaves, plus more for garnishing

½ cup coconut water

½ cup orange juice

1 tablespoon chia seeds

½ teaspoon ground ginger

½ teaspoon vanilla extract

1. Add the chopped beet, sliced banana, spinach, coconut water, orange juice, chia seeds, ginger, and vanilla extract to a blender.

2. Blend the ingredients on high until smooth and creamy.

3. If the smoothie is too thick, add more coconut water or orange juice until the smoothie reaches your preferred blood-like consistency.

4. Garnish with fresh greens and serve.

WORD TO THE WOEFUL

If you prefer a sweeter smoothie, you can add a small amount of honey, preferably from your local school's beekeeping club. To make the smoothie as cold as your crypt, add ice cubes to the blender.

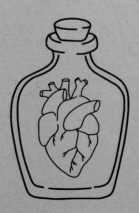

THE UNOFFICIAL WEDNESDAY COOKBOOK

PITTED DATES AND THE PENDULUM

When making this dish, imagine yourself as the protagonist of Edgar Allan Poe's "The Pit and the Pendulum." That pendulum is swinging above you, slicing closer and closer…. This appetizer will create a delicious sense of horrible tension sure to haunt your guests, even as they savor every bite.

Yield: 4 servings | Prep time: 10 minutes | Cook time: 15 to 20 minutes

12 pitted dates

4 ounces crumbled blue cheese (optional)

6 slices bacon, cut in half

toothpicks

1. Preheat the oven to 375°F and line a baking sheet with parchment paper.

2. Stuff each date with a small amount of blue cheese (if using) and wrap it with a half slice of bacon.

3. Secure each wrapped date with a toothpick.

4. Place the wrapped dates on the prepared baking sheet.

5. Bake for 15 to 20 minutes, or until the bacon is crispy.

6. Remove from the oven and let cool for a few minutes.

7. Serve warm.

WORD TO THE WOEFUL

This dish is often called "devils on horseback," a delightfully spooky little name for a delightfully delicious dish.

HONEY-ROASTED NUTS

Occasionally, strange uncles with an affinity for bees may surprise you at Nevermore. Instead of eating honeybees, perhaps your uncle would be willing to try some of these crunchy, sweet honey-roasted nuts. And if he's missing a little sting, give him a pinch.

Yield: 4 servings | Prep time: 5 to 10 minutes | Cook time: 10 to 12 minutes

2 cups raw cashews
¼ cup honey
2 tablespoons melted butter
1 teaspoon smoked paprika
½ teaspoon ground cumin
¼ teaspoon cayenne pepper
¼ teaspoon salt

1. Preheat the oven to 350°F and line a baking sheet with parchment paper.

2. Spread the raw cashews evenly on the prepared baking sheet.

3. In a small bowl, mix together the honey, melted butter, smoked paprika, cumin, cayenne pepper, and salt.

4. Drizzle the honey and spice mixture over the cashews and stir to coat evenly.

5. Roast the cashews in the oven for 10 to 12 minutes, or until they are golden brown and fragrant.

6. Remove the baking sheet from the oven and let the cashews cool for a few minutes.

7. Transfer the roasted cashews to a serving dish and let them cool completely.

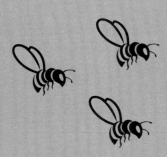

THE UNOFFICIAL WEDNESDAY COOKBOOK

CRYSTAL BALL ENERGY BITES

Feeling a little homesick? When you decide it's time to call home on your trusty crystal ball, try making these energy bites as a pick-me-up. Small but dense, they'll give you all the energy you need for quality family time, provided the call doesn't last *too* long.

Yield: 20 to 25 balls | Prep time: 15 minutes | Cook time: 30 minutes to chill

1 cup rolled oats

½ cup mixed nuts (such as almonds, pecans, and walnuts), chopped

½ cup dried fruit (such as dates, raisins, and apricots), chopped

¼ cup honey

¼ cup peanut butter

1 teaspoon vanilla extract

¼ teaspoon salt

shredded coconut, flaxseed, or white or black sesame seeds, for topping (optional)

1. In a large bowl, mix together the rolled oats, chopped nuts, and dried fruit.

2. In a separate bowl, whisk together the honey, peanut butter, vanilla extract, and salt until smooth.

3. Pour the peanut butter mixture over the oat mixture and stir until well combined.

4. Roll the mixture into small 1-inch balls and place them on a baking sheet lined with parchment paper.

5. If desired, roll the energy balls in shredded coconut, flaxseed, or sesame seeds until coated.

6. Place the energy balls in the refrigerator for at least 30 minutes to firm up.

WORD TO THE WOEFUL

Store your Crystal Ball Energy Bites in a container for up to a week as long as they are sealed airtight like any good mausoleum.

Dynamite Shrimp

A common family outing of the Addamses is, of course, blast fishing. Why go after a single fish when you could feast on a whole school? One of our favorite ways to share the bounty is with this shrimp dish. Be careful when eating—sometimes grenade rings can get stuck around a shrimp.

Yield: 4 servings | Prep time: 15 minutes | Cook time: 10 minutes

1 cup all-purpose flour

1 teaspoon salt

1 teaspoon pepper

1 teaspoon paprika

2 eggs, beaten

1½ cups panko bread crumbs

1 pound large shrimp, peeled and deveined

oil, for frying

rice, for serving

2 thinly sliced green onions, for garnishing

FOR THE DYNAMITE SAUCE

½ cup mayonnaise

2 tablespoons Thai sweet chili sauce

1 tablespoon honey

1 tablespoon sriracha sauce

1 tablespoon lime juice

1. In a small bowl, mix together the ingredients for the dynamite sauce and set aside.

2. In a separate bowl, combine the flour, salt, pepper, and paprika.

3. Place the beaten eggs in another bowl, and the panko bread crumbs in a third bowl.

4. Dredge each shrimp in the seasoned flour, then dip in the beaten eggs, and finally coat in the panko bread crumbs.

5. Heat about 1 inch of oil in a deep skillet over medium-high heat.

6. Fry the breaded shrimp in batches until golden brown, about 2 to 3 minutes per side.

7. Drain on paper towels to remove excess oil.

8. Toss the fried shrimp in the dynamite sauce until evenly coated.

9. Serve the shrimp over white rice and garnish with sliced green onions.

Date Night Caramel Corn

Let's set the scene. You're sitting with your date, who promises you a frightening time. It's dark. Perhaps there is some lovely lightning and terrifying thunder to set a perfectly dour mood. Then he presses play on the most terrifying thing you've ever seen—a pink-laden movie about a perky lawyer. As your eyes widen in terror, be sure to keep your grip on the popcorn bowl. You won't want to miss a single kernel of this treat.

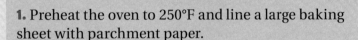

Yield: 6 to 8 people | Prep time: 15 to 20 minutes | Cook time: 1 hour

8 cups popped popcorn
1 cup brown sugar
½ cup butter
¼ cup corn syrup
½ teaspoon salt
½ teaspoon baking soda
1 teaspoon vanilla extract

1. Preheat the oven to 250°F and line a large baking sheet with parchment paper.

2. Spread the popcorn evenly on the prepared baking sheet.

3. In a medium saucepan, combine the brown sugar, butter, corn syrup, and salt. Cook over medium heat, stirring constantly, until the mixture comes to a boil.

4. Continue cooking the mixture for 5 minutes, stirring occasionally.

5. Remove the saucepan from the heat and stir in the baking soda and vanilla extract. The mixture will become frothy.

6. Pour the caramel sauce over the popcorn and stir gently to coat the popcorn evenly.

7. Bake the caramel corn in the oven for 1 hour, stirring every 15 minutes.

8. Remove the baking sheet from the oven and let the caramel corn cool completely.

9. Once the caramel corn is cool, break it into bite-size pieces and serve.

Sabotage Breadsticks

On the eve of the big tournament, a vampire had a terrible incident with garlic bread that forced her to resign from the team. Although unfortunate for her, it is a good idea to have a recipe for garlic bread on hand in case you also need to lightly sabotage a vampire. Garlic bread is also known as grissini, which reminds us of so many lovely little words. Grisly, grim, gristly, grimy. If you need to be more subtle with your subterfuge, refer to your snack as "grissini" when presenting it to your intended vampire.

Yield: 24 breadsticks | Prep time: 30 minutes, plus 1 to 2 hours to rise | Cook time: 15 to 20 minutes

2 cups all-purpose flour

1 teaspoon salt

1 teaspoon granulated sugar

1 tablespoon active dry yeast

¾ cup warm water

2 tablespoons plus ¼ cup olive oil, divided

FOR THE TOPPING

¼ cup grated parmesan cheese

¼ cup grated pecorino romano cheese

2 cloves garlic, minced

salt and pepper, to taste

1. In a large bowl, whisk together the flour, salt, sugar, and yeast until well combined.

2. Gradually add the warm water, stirring with a wooden spoon until a shaggy dough forms. Add the 2 tablespoons of olive oil and stir until combined.

3. Turn the dough out onto a floured surface and knead for 5 to 10 minutes, or until smooth and elastic.

4. Place the dough in a greased bowl, cover with a clean towel, and let rise in a warm, draft-free place for 1 to 2 hours, or until doubled in size.

5. Preheat the oven to 375°F.

6. In a small bowl, mix together the parmesan cheese, pecorino romano cheese, minced garlic, salt, and pepper.

7. Once the dough has risen, punch it down and roll it out on a lightly floured surface into a rectangle about ¼ inch thick.

8. Brush the surface of the dough with the remaining olive oil, then sprinkle the cheese and garlic mixture evenly over the dough.

9. Use a pizza cutter or sharp knife to cut the dough into thin strips about ½ inch wide.

10. Take each strip and twist it gently to create a spiral shape, then place the breadsticks onto a baking sheet lined with parchment paper.

11. Bake for 15 to 20 minutes, or until the breadsticks are golden brown and crispy.

12. Allow the breadsticks to cool for a few minutes before serving.

STONER FRUIT SALAD

The gorgons at Nevermore Academy certainly do have a stony reputation. If you want to perhaps find a crack in their rocky facade in order to make friends or, more likely, press them for information about mysterious headmistresses and secret societies, try this stoner fruit salad. Made from stone fruit picked just for them, it's sure to soften up any hard exteriors.

Yield: 4 to 6 servings | Prep time: 15 minutes | Cook time: 3 to 4 minutes

4 ripe peaches, halved and pitted

4 cups arugula

½ cup fresh mint leaves

½ cup crumbled blue cheese

¼ cup extra-virgin olive oil, plus more for brushing

2 tablespoons balsamic vinegar

1 tablespoon flaxseed, optional

salt and pepper, to taste

1. Preheat the grill to medium-high heat.

2. Brush the peach halves with a little bit of olive oil and season them with salt and pepper.

3. Place the peaches on the grill, cut-side down, and grill for 3 to 4 minutes, or until they are slightly charred and softened.

4. Remove the peaches from the grill and let them cool.

5. In a large mixing bowl, combine the arugula, mint leaves, and crumbled blue cheese.

6. Add the cooled peach halves to the mixing bowl and gently toss all the ingredients together.

7. In a small mixing bowl, whisk together the extra-virgin olive oil and balsamic vinegar until well combined.

8. Drizzle the vinaigrette over the salad and toss gently to coat. Top with flaxseed, if using.

9. Serve the salad immediately.

BLOOD MOON SALAD

Turning into a werewolf can be exhausting. To prep your fuzzy roommate for a night of fangs and fur, prepare this absolutely scrumptious salad for her before the full moon rises. If you sneak some bites, be sure to do so before the fangs come out.

Yield: 4 to 6 servings | Prep time: 15 to 20 minutes

4 cups fresh spinach leaves

2 blood oranges, peeled and sliced

½ cup crumbled goat cheese

½ cup pomegranate seeds

½ cup walnuts, roughly chopped

¼ cup extra-virgin olive oil

2 tablespoons freshly squeezed orange juice

1 tablespoon freshly squeezed lemon juice

1 teaspoon honey

salt and pepper, to taste

1. In a large mixing bowl, combine the spinach, sliced blood oranges, crumbled goat cheese, pomegranate seeds, and chopped walnuts.

2. In a small mixing bowl, whisk together the extra-virgin olive oil, orange juice, lemon juice, honey, salt, and pepper until well combined.

3. Drizzle the citrus dressing over the salad and toss gently to coat.

4. Serve the salad immediately.

WORD TO THE WOEFUL

A "blood moon" is another name for a total lunar eclipse. Various prophecies related to blood moons also exist—perhaps do some light reading while you enjoy your salad, or see if you can create your own blood moon ritual.

DEVILED EGGS

Sometimes when you need help with your own hellish crusade, it's time to turn the darkest of all dark ones. And this crowd-pleasing appetizer is a staple for a reason—temptation tastes delicious.

Yield: 6 servings | Prep time: 15 minutes | Cook time: 10 to 12 minutes

6 large eggs

¼ cup mayonnaise

1 teaspoon Dijon mustard

¼ teaspoon paprika, plus more for garnishing

salt and pepper, to taste

¼ cup shredded cheddar cheese

1 thinly sliced green onion, for garnishing

1. Place the eggs in a pot of cold water and bring to a boil over high heat.

2. Once the water boils, cover the pot and remove it from the heat. Let the eggs sit in the hot water for 10 to 12 minutes.

3. Remove the eggs from the pot and place them in a bowl of ice water. Let the eggs cool for 5 minutes.

4. Peel the eggs and cut them in half lengthwise. Remove the yolks and place them in a small mixing bowl.

5. Add the mayonnaise, Dijon mustard, paprika, salt, and pepper to the mixing bowl with the egg yolks. Mash everything together until well combined.

6. Spoon the mixture back into the egg white halves.

7. Sprinkle the shredded cheddar cheese on top of the deviled eggs, then dust with a little more paprika.

8. Garnish with thinly sliced green onions.

9. Serve the deviled eggs immediately or refrigerate until ready to serve.

THE UNOFFICIAL WEDNESDAY COOKBOOK

TAXIDERMIED MUSHROOMS

Departed friends never really have to leave us, and what better way to keep them around than mounting them on a wall? When you want to practice your skills but have only tragically living animal friends, try stuffing some mushrooms instead. A tasty and practical way to bide your time as you wait for some more appropriate subjects.

Yield: 4 to 6 servings | Prep time: 20 minutes | Cook time: 20 to 25 minutes

16 large mushrooms, stems removed

¼ cup bread crumbs

¼ cup grated parmesan cheese

2 cloves garlic, minced

2 tablespoons fresh chopped parsley

2 tablespoons fresh chopped basil

¼ cup olive oil

salt and pepper, to taste

1. Preheat the oven to 375°F.

2. Finely chop the mushroom stems and set aside.

3. In a mixing bowl, combine the chopped mushroom stems, bread crumbs, parmesan cheese, garlic, parsley, basil, salt, and pepper.

4. Stuff the mushroom caps with the bread crumb mixture.

5. Place the stuffed mushrooms in a baking dish and drizzle them with the olive oil.

6. Bake the mushrooms for 20 to 25 minutes, or until the cheese is melted and the mushrooms are tender.

7. Remove the mushrooms from the oven and let them cool for a few minutes before serving.

CRACKED PEPPER CRYPT CRACKERS

Of all the cozy places to dine, our favorite is of course a forgotten and lightly haunted crypt. It's only polite to bring enough to share with the departed souls around you, and they'll be howling for more of these crispy snacks. Perhaps if they like them enough, they'll do you a favor and haunt your dorm room. Studying always goes more smoothly with a soothing soundtrack of rattling chains in the background, doesn't it?

> Yield: 30 to 35 crackers | Prep time: 15 minutes, plus 30 to 60 minutes to chill | Cook time: 15 to 18 minutes

1½ cups all-purpose flour

½ teaspoon salt

½ teaspoon baking powder

½ teaspoon freshly ground pepper

½ teaspoon garlic powder

¼ teaspoon cayenne pepper

4 tablespoons unsalted butter, chilled and cubed

2 cups grated sharp cheddar cheese

½ cup cold water

salt, to taste

1. Preheat the oven to 350°F. Line 2 baking sheets with parchment paper.

2. In a large mixing bowl, whisk together the flour, salt, baking powder, pepper, garlic powder, and cayenne pepper.

3. Using a pastry blender or your hands, cut in the cold butter until the mixture resembles coarse sand.

4. Add the grated cheddar cheese and mix well.

5. Gradually add the cold water as needed, 1 tablespoon at a time, mixing until the dough comes together.

6. Form the dough into a disc and wrap it in plastic wrap. Chill the dough for 30 minutes to an hour.

7. On a lightly floured surface, roll out the dough to about ⅛-inch thickness.

8. Cut the dough into 1-inch squares using a sharp knife or pizza cutter.

9. Place the crackers on the prepared baking sheet and prick each one with a fork. Sprinkle with salt.

10. Bake for 15 to 18 minutes, or until the crackers are golden brown and crisp.

11. Allow the crackers to cool on the baking sheet for a few minutes before transferring them to a wire rack to cool completely.

12. Serve the crackers at room temperature.

GUILLOTINE SALAD

Across all iterations of the Addams family, Wednesday has always been very fond of a guillotine (including as an accessory to her favorite doll, Marie Antoinette). As a tribute to her favorite practical tool, this chopped salad would be frightfully fun to make with a miniature guillotine. If your own kitchen guillotine is rusted, a regular kitchen knife will do. Your friends are sure to lose their heads over this healthy snack.

Yield: 4 servings | Prep time: 20 minutes

1 pound store-bought pulled pork

1 head romaine lettuce, chopped

½ head red cabbage, thinly sliced

1 red bell pepper, thinly sliced

1 cup corn kernels

1 cucumber, thinly sliced

1 serrano pepper, chopped

1 avocado, sliced

½ cup crumbled feta cheese

¼ cup chopped fresh cilantro

salt and pepper, to taste

FOR THE DRESSING

¼ cup olive oil

2 tablespoons apple cider vinegar

1 tablespoon honey

1 teaspoon Dijon mustard

1 clove garlic, minced

salt and pepper, to taste

1. Preheat the oven to 350°F. Heat the pulled pork in the oven for about 10 minutes, or until warmed through.

2. In the bottom of a large salad bowl, arrange the chopped romaine lettuce.

3. Create rows of thinly sliced red cabbage, bell pepper, corn, cucumber, chopped serrano pepper, and warm pulled pork on top of the lettuce.

4. Top the salad with sliced avocado, crumbled feta cheese, and chopped cilantro.

5. In a small bowl, whisk together the olive oil, apple cider vinegar, honey, Dijon mustard, minced garlic, salt, and pepper to make the dressing.

6. Drizzle the dressing over the salad, and toss everything together until well combined.

7. Season with salt and pepper to taste.

WORD TO THE WOEFUL

If you fear spice and heat or are simply not a fan of serranos, try substituting a milder pepper like a bell pepper or poblano pepper. Also try switching up the order of the rows to add some visual interest. We do so value the aesthetically pleasing.

FINGER FOOD

We simply couldn't let this cookbook go without a tribute to Wednesday's right-hand man. He's always ready to snap to attention. To honor our beloved friend, let's give him a hand. Or perhaps, just a few fingers?

Yield: 4 to 6 servings | Prep time: 10 minutes | Cook time: 10 minutes

6 hot dogs

6 hot dog buns

ketchup

1. Preheat the oven to 350°F.

2. Cut a small section off the end of each hot dog to create the look of a fingernail.

3. Use a paring knife to create knuckle-like cuts in the hot dogs, about 3 to 4 cuts per dog.

4. Boil the hot dogs for 5 to 7 minutes or until cooked through.

5. While the hot dogs are boiling, place the hot dog buns in the oven to toast for about 5 minutes. Once the hot dogs are cooked, place them in the buns.

6. Squeeze ketchup over the hot dogs to resemble blood and serve.

WORD TO THE WOEFUL

We know Wednesday would prefer to see the most realistic fingers possible. To make the knuckles look more defined, gently bend the hot dogs in the areas you cut before boiling. After enjoying the presentation of your bloody fingers, feel free to prepare the hot dogs to your preferences: add additional toppings like mustard, relish, or sauerkraut.

THE UNOFFICIAL WEDNESDAY COOKBOOK

Raven Wings

At Nevermore Academy, Edgar Allan Poe is always on our minds and in our hearts. If you wish to do so, you may choose to endear yourself to the school by making these delicious Raven Wings. Of course, we very rarely recommend social events. Instead, eat them all by yourself one midnight dreary. Don't be surprised if your fellow classmates follow the aroma and ask for some by tap, tap, tapping on your chamber door.

Yield: 4 to 6 servings | Prep time: 10 minutes | Cook time: 30 to 40 minutes

2 tablespoons olive oil
2 teaspoons smoked paprika
2 teaspoons garlic powder
salt and pepper, to taste
2 pounds chicken wings
1 cup barbecue sauce

✕

1. Preheat the oven to 425°F.

2. Line a baking sheet with aluminum foil and place a wire rack on top.

3. In a small bowl, whisk together the olive oil, smoked paprika, garlic powder, salt, and pepper.

4. Pat the chicken wings dry with paper towels and place them on the wire rack.

5. Brush the chicken wings with the spice mixture and bake in the oven for 25 to 30 minutes.

6. While the chicken wings are baking, heat the barbecue sauce in a small saucepan over medium heat.

7. Once the chicken wings are cooked through, remove them from the oven and brush them with the barbecue sauce.

8. Return the chicken wings to the oven and bake for an additional 5 to 10 minutes or until the barbecue sauce is sticky and caramelized.

9. Serve the chicken wings hot with additional barbecue sauce on the side.

WORD TO THE WOEFUL

We love the sound of biting into something with a crunch. For extra-crispy wings, pat them dry with paper towels and let them sit in the fridge for at least an hour before baking. We also love to make people cry a bit. To make spicier wings to encourage tears, add a pinch of cayenne pepper to the spice mixture.

GOTHIC GUACAMOLE

Beneath the light of a full blood moon in between battling demons and crazed botany teachers, you may need a delicious snack. This is one of our favorites—green like a monster, flavorful as the best potions, and great with chips.

Yield: 2 cups | Prep time: 15 minutes

3 ripe avocados

1 small onion, diced

2 cloves garlic, minced

1 to 2 jalapeño chiles, seeded and minced

1 medium tomato, diced

1 tablespoon lime juice

1 teaspoon ground cumin

salt and pepper, to taste

fresh chopped cilantro, for topping (optional)

1. Cut the avocados in half and remove the pit. Scoop the flesh into a bowl.

2. Mash the avocado with a fork or potato masher until desired consistency is reached.

3. Add the onion, garlic, jalapeños, tomato, lime juice, cumin, salt, and pepper to the bowl with the mashed avocado.

4. Mix all the ingredients together until well combined.

5. Taste and adjust seasoning as needed.

6. If using, top with fresh cilantro before serving with chips.

THE UNOFFICIAL WEDNESDAY COOKBOOK

PLATS DU WOE: MAIN DISHES

I pray you, be seated and sup how you please. You will I trust, excuse me that I do not join you, but I have dined already, and I do not sup.

—Bram Stoker, *Dracula*

SKEWERED SIREN

Nothing is quite as invigorating as a fencing match between new foes or old friends. Take up your saber (or in this case, skewers) and stab away....

Yield: 4 servings | Prep time: 15 minutes | Cook time: 10 to 12 minutes

¼ cup olive oil

2 cloves garlic, minced

2 tablespoons lemon juice

1 tablespoon honey

salt and pepper, to taste

1 pound salmon fillets, cut into cubes

2 small zucchini, sliced into rounds

1 small eggplant, sliced into rounds

1 cup cherry tomatoes

skewers

1. Soak the skewers in water for at least 30 minutes.

2. Preheat your grill to medium-high heat.

3. In a small bowl, whisk together the olive oil, garlic, lemon juice, honey, salt, and pepper.

4. Thread the salmon, zucchini, eggplant, and cherry tomatoes onto the skewers, alternating between the ingredients.

5. Brush the skewers with the marinade.

6. Grill the skewers for 10 to 12 minutes, flipping once halfway through, or until the salmon is cooked through and the vegetables are tender and lightly charred.

7. Remove the skewers from the grill and serve hot.

WORD TO THE WOEFUL

If you are saving your nice sabers and instead using wooden skewers, ensure that you soak them in water for at least 30 minutes before using them. Although we occasionally enjoy seeing flames, we do not want the wooden skewers to burn on the grill.

HONEY-SOY CHICKEN THIGHS

The beekeeping club is a small but vital population of the Nevermore Academy. Without an astute apiarist, Wednesday would find herself in some incredibly sticky situations. In honor of our friend and his bees, we created this honey-soy chicken meal. Invite your local beekeeping club. You never know when they'll come to your rescue, as hummers always keep their word.

Yield: 4 servings | Prep time: 10 minutes | Cook time: 20 to 25 minutes

¼ cup soy sauce

2 tablespoons honey

2 tablespoons olive oil

2 cloves garlic, minced

1 tablespoon grated fresh ginger

1 tablespoon sesame oil

4 bone-in, skin-on chicken thighs

1 tablespoon sesame seeds

2 green onions, thinly sliced

1. Preheat the oven to 425°F.

2. In a small bowl, whisk together the soy sauce, honey, olive oil, garlic, ginger, and sesame oil.

3. Place the chicken thighs in a baking dish, skin-side up, and brush with the marinade.

4. Bake the chicken thighs in the oven for 25 to 30 minutes, or until the chicken is cooked through and the skin is crispy and golden brown.

5. While the chicken is baking, toast the sesame seeds in a dry pan over medium heat until lightly browned.

6. Remove the chicken from the oven and let it rest for a few minutes.

7. Sprinkle the sesame seeds and sliced green onions over the chicken thighs.

8. Serve hot.

Spaghetti Al Nero

How do we honor a fallen friend? In the case of Wednesday's beloved childhood pet scorpion, we turn him into spaghetti. Because many people are not yet acclimated to the taste of scorpion venom, we've instead created this pasta dish which is a symphony of our dearly departed arachnid's favorite things: his favorite color (the happiest shade of black) and his favorite flavor (plenty of garlic).

Yield: 4 servings | Prep time: 5 minutes | Cook time: 15 minutes

1 pound black (squid ink) spaghetti

2 tablespoons olive oil

4 cloves garlic, minced

½ teaspoon lemon zest

½ teaspoon pepper

½ cup freshly grated parmesan cheese, plus more for garnishing

¼ cup chopped fresh basil leaves, plus more for garnishing

salt, to taste

1. Cook the black spaghetti in a large pot of boiling salted water according to package instructions, until al dente.

2. While the spaghetti is cooking, heat the olive oil in a large saucepan over medium heat.

3. Add the minced garlic to the pan and cook for 1 to 2 minutes, until fragrant.

4. Add the lemon zest and pepper to the pan and stir to combine.

5. When the spaghetti is cooked, drain it and reserve 1 cup of the cooking water.

6. Add the cooked spaghetti to the saucepan with the garlic and lemon pepper sauce.

7. Toss the spaghetti with the sauce, adding a splash of the reserved cooking water if necessary to loosen the sauce.

8. Add the grated parmesan cheese and chopped basil leaves to the pan and toss again to combine.

9. Season the spaghetti with salt, to taste.

10. Serve the black spaghetti hot, garnished with additional parmesan cheese and basil leaves, if desired.

WORD TO THE WOEFUL

Save some of the cooking water from the spaghetti. Adding it to the sauce will create a creamy texture. Black spaghetti can be found at most specialty grocery stores or online, but if you find yourself bereft of such a luxury, regular spaghetti works fine. Just be sure to think dark thoughts while consuming.

SECRET SOCIETY RATATOUILLE

Shh! Discretion is the most important virtue to a member of a secret society. If perhaps you need to give a signal to another society member without being spotted, try this deliciously inconspicuous meal. Ratatouille is a healthy mixture of tomatoes and eggplant, both of which are nightshade vegetables. Those within the society will instantly recognize this as an indication of membership, while those not within the society will simply enjoy a mouthwatering meal.

Yield: 4 to 6 servings | Prep time: 20 minutes | Cook time: 55 to 65 minutes

1 large eggplant, sliced into rounds

2 zucchini, sliced into rounds

1 red bell pepper, sliced

1 yellow onion, sliced

4 medium tomatoes, sliced

4 cloves garlic, minced

2 tablespoons tomato paste

1 teaspoon dried thyme

1 teaspoon dried oregano

2 tablespoons olive oil

¼ cup chopped fresh basil leaves, for garnishing

salt and pepper, to taste

1. Preheat the oven to 375°F.

2. In a large baking dish, arrange the sliced eggplant, zucchini, red bell pepper, onion, and tomatoes in a circular pattern, alternating the vegetables.

3. In a small bowl, mix together the minced garlic, tomato paste, thyme, oregano, salt, and pepper. Spread this mixture over the top of the vegetables.

4. Drizzle the olive oil over the vegetables.

5. Cover the baking dish with foil and bake for 45 to 50 minutes, or until the vegetables are tender.

6. Remove the foil and bake for an additional 10 to 15 minutes, or until the vegetables are lightly browned on top.

7. Sprinkle chopped fresh basil over the top of the ratatouille before serving.

WORD TO THE WOEFUL
These particular nightshades are not deadly, so this meal is safe for allies and the unknowing.

Amontillado Risotto

One of the school's most illustrious alumni, Edgar Allan Poe inspired the no-rules boat race at Nevermore. In one of his most famous short stories "The Cask of Amontillado," he describes one of the most deliciously devious revenge plots. In case you want to get a similar flavor of revenge without having to find any pesky catacombs in which to entomb an enemy, try this rice dish. It may not be as deadly as a revenge scheme, but it will be just as satisfying.

Yield: 4 to 6 servings | Prep time: 10 minutes | Cook time: 30 to 35 minutes

6 cups chicken or vegetable broth

2 tablespoons olive oil

1 onion, finely chopped

2 cups arborio rice

1 cup amontillado sherry

2 cups sliced mushrooms

½ cup grated parmesan cheese

salt and pepper, to taste

chopped fresh parsley, for garnishing

1. In a medium saucepan, bring the broth to a simmer and keep warm over low heat.

2. In a large skillet, heat the olive oil over medium heat. Add the onion and cook until softened, about 5 minutes.

3. Add the rice and stir until it is coated with the oil and onions, about 2 minutes.

4. Add the amontillado sherry and stir until it is absorbed by the rice, about 2 minutes.

5. Add ½ cup of the warm broth to the rice and stir until it is absorbed. Continue adding broth, ½ cup at a time, stirring constantly, until the rice is tender and creamy, about 20 to 25 minutes.

6. While the rice is cooking, sauté the sliced mushrooms in a separate pan until they are golden brown.

7. When the rice is done, stir in the sautéed mushrooms, grated parmesan cheese, and salt and pepper to taste.

8. Serve the risotto hot, garnished with chopped fresh parsley.

WORD TO THE WOEFUL

When faced with a particularly frustrating adversary, remember the protagonist's family motto: *Nemo me impune lacessit (No one provokes me with impunity)*. If the motto doesn't work to make you feel better, remember that Poe has myriad suggestions for dealing with enemies. We can learn so much from literature.

GOLD-BUG POTATOES

Like "The Cask of Amontillado," "The Gold-Bug" by Edgar Allan Poe serves as inspiration for Nevermore's competing teams. Instead of solving ciphers and traveling through an island for a lost fortune, try enjoying a much more simple and constant treasure: potatoes.

Yield: 4 servings | Prep time: 10 minutes | Cook time: 40 to 45 minutes

4 medium Yukon
Gold potatoes

2 tablespoons olive oil

1 tablespoon fresh
rosemary, finely chopped

salt and pepper, to taste

✕

1. Preheat the oven to 425°F.

2. Rinse and scrub the potatoes under cold running water. Dry them well.

3. Place a potato on a cutting board and make thin, evenly spaced cuts into the potato, being careful not to slice all the way through. Repeat with the remaining potatoes.

4. Place the potatoes in a baking dish or cast-iron skillet.

5. Drizzle the olive oil over the potatoes, making sure it gets into the cuts.

6. Sprinkle the chopped rosemary over the potatoes.

7. Season the potatoes with salt and pepper.

8. Bake for 40 to 45 minutes, or until the potatoes are tender on the inside and crispy on the outside.

WORD TO THE WOEFUL

To ensure the crispiest of potatoes, heat up your cast-iron skillet before adding the potatoes. Don't you love the sound of sizzling?

FUR-FRIENDLY STEAK TARTARE

Wednesday's roommate's favorite scent is her steak tartare candle. When you need to sway your werewolf roommate to join your crusade, try convincing her with this edible version of her beloved aroma. Surely she will see your side, though she may have trouble verbally agreeing while devouring this delicious delicacy.

Yield: 4 to 6 servings | Prep time: 20 minutes

1 pound beef tenderloin, finely chopped

2 tablespoons capers, drained and chopped

2 tablespoons cornichons or small dill pickles, drained and chopped

2 tablespoons Dijon mustard

1 tablespoon Worcestershire sauce

1 tablespoon minced shallot

2 tablespoons chopped parsley

1 egg yolk

salt and pepper, to taste

toasted bread or crackers, for serving

1. In a mixing bowl, combine the beef, capers, cornichons, Dijon mustard, Worcestershire sauce, shallot, and parsley. Mix well.

2. Season the mixture with salt and pepper to taste.

3. Divide the mixture into individual portions and shape them into round disks.

4. Using the back of a spoon, make a small well in the center of each disk. Add the egg yolk to the well.

5. Serve the steak tartare with toasted bread or crackers.

WORD TO THE WOEFUL

Remember, accidental poisoning can ruin an occasion. Consuming raw or undercooked meats, poultry, seafood, shellfish, or eggs may increase your risk of foodborne illness, especially if you have certain medical conditions. Make sure to use high-quality, fresh ingredients and practice proper food safety when preparing and serving raw egg dishes.

POPCORN "RATTLESNAKE" BITES

A beloved father-daughter tradition of flaying rattlesnakes led to the creation of this tasty treat. If rattlesnakes are not readily available to you, try this less venomous chicken version. Scrumptious, but still with a little bite.

Yield: 4 to 6 servings | Prep time: 15 minutes | Cook time: 15 minutes

1 cup all-purpose flour

1 teaspoon paprika

1 teaspoon garlic powder

1 teaspoon onion powder

½ teaspoon salt

¼ teaspoon pepper

2 eggs

2 tablespoons milk

vegetable oil, for frying

1 pound boneless, skinless chicken breasts, cut into bite-size pieces

1. In a shallow bowl, mix together the flour, paprika, garlic powder, onion powder, salt, and pepper.

2. In another shallow bowl, whisk together the eggs and milk.

3. Heat the vegetable oil in a large frying pan over medium-high heat. Use enough oil to cover the chicken pieces.

4. Working in batches, coat the chicken pieces in the flour mixture, then dip them in the egg mixture and coat them in the flour mixture again. Shake off any excess flour.

5. Carefully place the chicken pieces in the hot oil and cook until golden brown and cooked through, about 3 to 4 minutes per batch.

6. Using a slotted spoon, transfer the chicken pieces to a paper towel–lined plate to drain any excess oil.

7. Serve immediately, with your favorite dipping sauce.

Gorgon-zola and Pear Salad

Perhaps your roommate has some warm and fuzzy feelings toward a young Gorgon at school. Perhaps she will not stop talking about him and you would like some peace and quiet for once. How else are you supposed to solve a complex mystery surrounding the school? Try making this enticing meal that the two sweethearts can take on a picnic—far away from you and your solitude.

Yield: 4 to 6 servings | Prep time: 10 minutes

¼ cup olive oil

2 tablespoons balsamic vinegar

1 tablespoon honey

1 teaspoon Dijon mustard

salt and pepper, to taste

6 cups mixed greens

1 ripe pear, thinly sliced

½ cup crumbled Gorgonzola cheese

½ cup chopped walnuts

¼ cup thinly sliced red onion

1. In a small bowl, whisk together the olive oil, balsamic vinegar, honey, Dijon mustard, salt, and pepper to make the dressing.

2. In a large salad bowl, toss the mixed greens with the dressing until well coated.

3. Add the sliced pear, crumbled Gorgonzola cheese, chopped walnuts, and thinly sliced red onion on top of the mixed greens.

4. Toss the salad until all ingredients are evenly distributed.

5. Serve immediately.

WORD TO THE WOEFUL

What a wonderful time to practice your knife skills. Slicing the pear thinly ensures that it can be evenly distributed throughout the salad.

KETCHUP-SPLATTERED MEATLOAF

If your strange and insistent uncle requires more than the previous snack we recommended, offer him this appetizing dinner that makes good use of the ketchup he's been inhaling. It also can appear a bit like blood, which will hopefully remind him of home and bring him some comfort.

Yield: 4 to 6 servings | Prep time: 15 minutes | Cook time: 60 to 75 minutes

1½ pounds ground beef
½ cup bread crumbs
½ cup milk
1 egg
½ onion, finely chopped
¼ cup ketchup
1 tablespoon Worcestershire sauce
1 teaspoon salt
½ teaspoon pepper

FOR THE GLAZE
¼ cup ketchup
2 tablespoons brown sugar

1. Preheat the oven to 350°F.

2. In a large bowl, mix together the ground beef, bread crumbs, milk, egg, onion, ketchup, Worcestershire sauce, salt, and pepper.

3. Shape the mixture into a loaf and place it in a baking dish.

4. In a small bowl, mix together the ¼ cup of ketchup and brown sugar to make the glaze. Spread the mixture over the top of the meatloaf.

5. Bake the meatloaf in the oven for 60 to 75 minutes, or until fully cooked.

6. Let the meatloaf rest for 10 minutes before slicing and serving.

Harvest Festival Burger

Occasionally, one may find oneself craving a classic yet tasty repast, the likes of which can be found at the local Harvest Festival. If you do not want to subject yourself to the social expectations of whimsy, make your own burger. Just as good, and no need for tiresome conversations, fanciful games, or—shudder the thought—fun.

Yield: 4 servings | Prep time: 10 minutes | Cook time: 10 to 15 minutes

1 pound ground beef

4 burger buns

4 slices of provolone cheese, optional

¼ cup prepared pesto, optional

lettuce and tomato slices, for serving

salt and pepper, to taste

1. Preheat the grill to medium-high heat.

2. Divide the ground beef into 4 equal portions and shape each portion into a patty. Season each patty with salt and pepper on both sides.

3. Grill the burgers for 4 to 5 minutes per side or until desired level of doneness is achieved.

4. While the burgers are cooking, toast the buns on the grill or in the oven.

5. Once the burgers are almost cooked, top each patty with a slice of provolone cheese, if using, and let it melt.

6. Spread pesto onto the bottom of each toasted bun, if using. Add lettuce and tomato slices on top of the pesto.

7. Place a cooked burger patty on each bottom bun and top with the other half of the bun.

Goo Goo-lash Muck

Music can soothe the savage beast, but why would you want to? Let the beasts dance! In honor of Wednesday's iconic routine, whip up this mouthwatering meal. I think you know which song to play while you do.

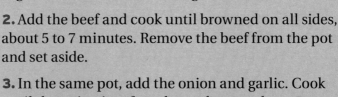

Yield: 4 to 6 servings | Prep time: 20 minutes | Cook time: 2 to 2½ hours

1 tablespoon vegetable oil

2 pounds beef chuck or stew meat, cut into bite-size pieces

1 large onion, diced

2 cloves garlic, minced

2 tablespoons sweet paprika

1 teaspoon caraway seeds

2 tablespoons tomato paste

2 cups beef broth

1 (14.5-ounce) can diced tomatoes

2 bay leaves

salt and pepper, to taste

cooked egg noodles or potatoes, for serving (optional)

1. In a large Dutch oven or heavy pot, heat the vegetable oil over medium-high heat.

2. Add the beef and cook until browned on all sides, about 5 to 7 minutes. Remove the beef from the pot and set aside.

3. In the same pot, add the onion and garlic. Cook until the onion is soft and translucent, about 5 minutes.

4. Add the sweet paprika, caraway seeds, and tomato paste. Cook for 1 to 2 minutes, stirring constantly.

5. Add the beef broth, diced tomatoes (with their juices), and bay leaves. Stir to combine.

6. Add the browned beef back to the pot. Bring the mixture to a simmer, then reduce the heat to low.

7. Cover and let the goulash simmer for 1½ to 2 hours, or until the beef is tender and the sauce has thickened.

8. Season with salt and pepper to taste.

9. Serve the goulash over cooked egg noodles or potatoes, if desired.

THE UNOFFICIAL WEDNESDAY COOKBOOK

JEKYLL AND HYDE SWEET AND SOUR PORK

In the classic gothic novella by Robert Louis Stevenson, we meet a man who hides an evil alter ego just below his surface. We do love celebrating the monstrous within us all, but be careful. Sometimes the most unforgivingly murderous creatures can hide under a familiar barista's apron.

Yield: 4 servings | Prep time: 15 minutes | Cook time: 20 minutes

1 pound pork tenderloin, cut into bite-size pieces

½ cup plus 1 tablespoon cornstarch, divided

¼ cup vegetable oil

1 green bell pepper, diced

1 red bell pepper, diced

1 onion, diced

1 carrot, diced

¼ cup white vinegar

¼ cup brown sugar

¼ cup ketchup

2 tablespoons soy sauce

½ cup pineapple chunks

¼ cup sliced green onions, for garnish

1. In a large bowl, toss the pork pieces with ½ cup of cornstarch until fully coated.

2. Heat the vegetable oil in a large skillet or wok over medium-high heat. Add the pork and cook until browned and crispy, about 5 to 7 minutes. Remove the pork from the skillet and set aside.

3. Add the diced green and red bell peppers, onion, and carrot to the same skillet and cook until slightly softened, about 3 to 5 minutes.

4. In a small bowl, whisk together the white vinegar, brown sugar, ketchup, soy sauce, and 1 tablespoon of cornstarch.

5. Add the pineapple chunks and sauce to the skillet and bring to a boil, stirring constantly. Reduce the heat to low and let simmer for 5 minutes until the sauce has thickened.

6. Add the pork back into the skillet and toss to coat with the sauce.

7. Serve the sweet and sour pork hot, garnished with sliced green onions.

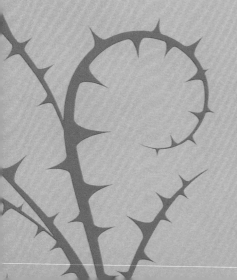

THANKSGIVING-INSPIRED TURKEY PINWHEELS

In the 1993 film *Addams Family Values*, Wednesday famously presents her strong opinions on Thanksgiving with flaming arrows and threats of scalping. Although we agree with her on the general rule of "do not trust the pilgrims," we do enjoy a turkey pinwheel. As a reminder: do not break bread with pilgrims, perky camp counselors, or particularly bubbly blondes.

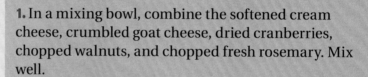

Yield: 4 to 6 servings | Prep time: 20 minutes | Cook time: 30 minutes to chill

8 ounces cream cheese, softened

¼ cup crumbled goat cheese

¼ cup dried cranberries

¼ cup chopped walnuts

1 teaspoon chopped fresh rosemary

4 large spinach tortillas

8 to 10 ounces sliced turkey breast

salt and pepper, to taste

1. In a mixing bowl, combine the softened cream cheese, crumbled goat cheese, dried cranberries, chopped walnuts, and chopped fresh rosemary. Mix well.

2. Spread a generous layer of the cheese mixture evenly over each spinach tortilla.

3. Layer thinly sliced turkey breast over the cheese mixture, making sure to cover the entire tortilla.

4. Sprinkle salt and pepper over the turkey slices.

5. Tightly roll up each tortilla, being careful not to tear it.

6. Chill the rolled tortillas in the fridge for at least 30 minutes.

7. Cut each chilled tortilla roll into 1-inch-thick slices to make the pinwheels.

8. Serve the pinwheels chilled.

THE UNOFFICIAL WEDNESDAY COOKBOOK

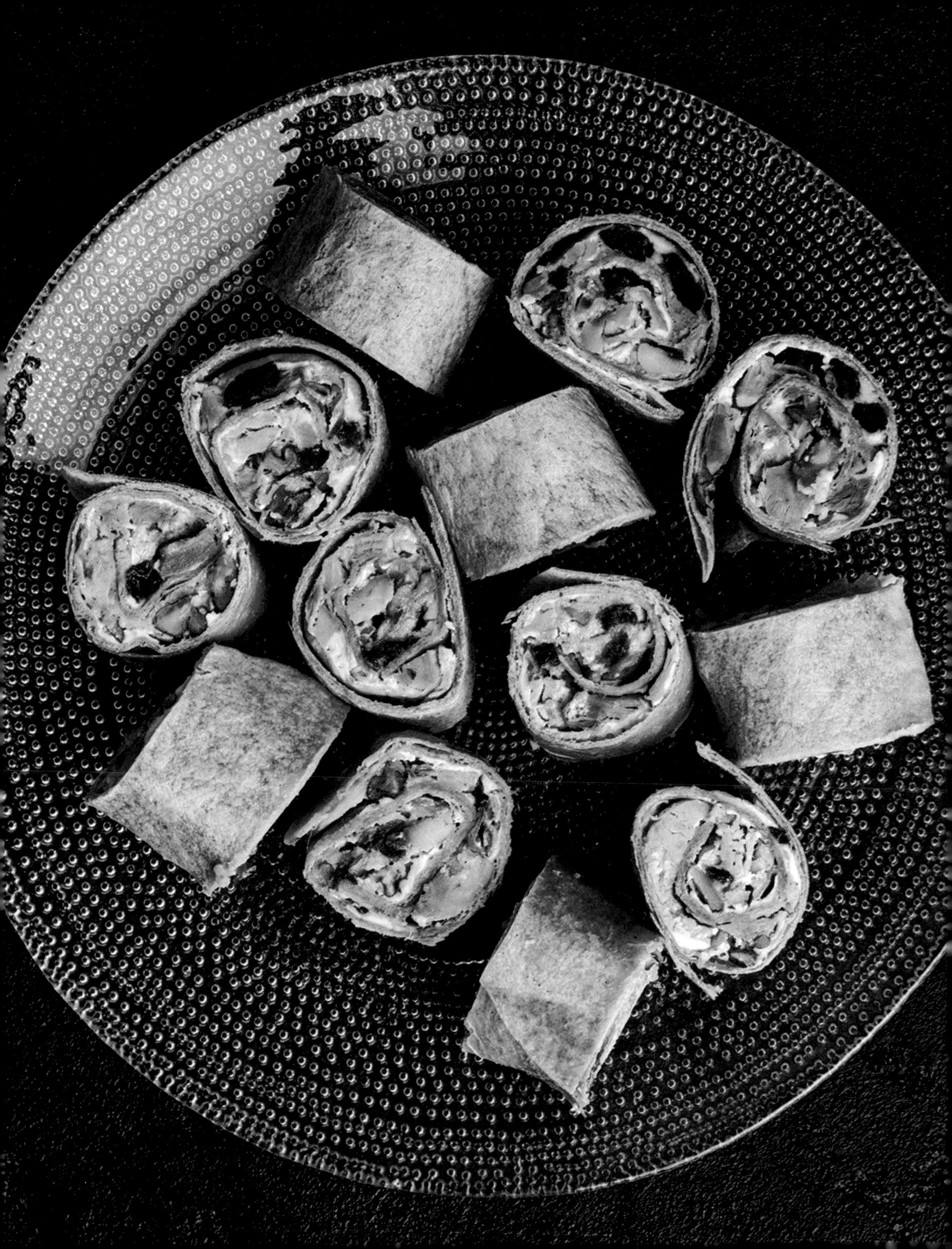

Slow Cooker Cauldron Chili con Carne

Have you been accused of being a witch? How lovely to be recognized by your community for your work. If you'd like to celebrate, create this delectable chili con carne in your favorite cauldron. A slow cooker will also work, of course.

Yield: 8 to 10 servings | Prep time: 15 to 20 minutes | Cook time: 6 to 8 hours on low; 3 to 4 hours on high

2 pounds ground beef

1 onion, chopped

4 cloves garlic, minced

2 bell peppers, chopped

2 (14.5-ounce) cans diced tomatoes

1 (6-ounce) can tomato paste

1 (15-ounce) can kidney beans, drained and rinsed

1 (15-ounce) can black beans, drained and rinsed

2 cups beef broth

2 tablespoons chili powder

1 tablespoon ground cumin

1 teaspoon paprika

1 teaspoon salt

½ teaspoon pepper

¼ teaspoon cayenne pepper

2 carrots, peeled and chopped

1 cup frozen corn

shredded cheese, for serving

sour cream, for serving

green onions, chopped, for serving

1. In a large skillet, cook the ground beef over medium-high heat until browned, breaking it up with a spoon as it cooks. Drain the excess fat and transfer the beef to a slow cooker.

2. Add the onion, garlic, bell peppers, diced tomatoes, tomato paste, kidney beans, black beans, beef broth, chili powder, cumin, paprika, salt, pepper, and cayenne pepper to the slow cooker.

3. Stir everything together until well combined. Add the chopped carrots and corn, and stir again.

4. Cover the slow cooker and cook on low heat for 6 to 8 hours or on high heat for 3 to 4 hours, or until the vegetables are tender and the flavors are well combined.

5. Once the chili is ready, serve it hot with shredded cheese, sour cream, and chopped green onions.

BLOOD RED TOMATO SOUP AND GRILLED CHEESE CROUTONS

Don't you love it when the weather is just ideal? When there is a cold snap in the air and the sky is gray, with perhaps a terrible storm brewing? How perfectly grim! While you're enjoying the gloomy day, whip up this satisfying pairing.

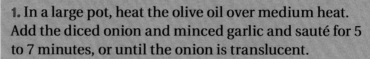

Yield: 4 servings | Prep time: 10 minutes | Cook time: 30 minutes

2 tablespoons olive oil

1 medium yellow onion, diced

4 cloves garlic, minced

2 (28-ounce) cans crushed tomatoes

4 cups vegetable broth

¼ cup heavy cream

4 slices bread

2 tablespoons unsalted butter, at room temperature

4 slices cheddar cheese

salt and pepper, to taste

1. In a large pot, heat the olive oil over medium heat. Add the diced onion and minced garlic and sauté for 5 to 7 minutes, or until the onion is translucent.

2. Add the crushed tomatoes and vegetable broth to the pot and stir to combine. Season with salt and pepper to taste.

3. Increase the heat to high and bring the soup to a boil. Once boiling, reduce the heat to low and let simmer for 20 to 25 minutes, stirring occasionally.

4. Using an immersion blender or transferring the soup to a blender, puree the soup until smooth. Stir in the heavy cream and adjust the seasoning if necessary.

5. Preheat a pan over medium heat. Butter one side of each slice of bread and place the cheese slices on the non-buttered side of 2 slices of bread. Top with the remaining 2 slices of bread, buttered side facing out.

6. Place the sandwiches in the pan and cook until the bread is golden brown and the cheese is melted, flipping once.

7. Cut the grilled cheese sandwiches into cubes to make croutons.

8. Serve the soup hot, garnished with grilled cheese croutons.

THE UNOFFICIAL WEDNESDAY COOKBOOK

DROWNED CHILAQUILES

Sirens are known for their beautiful voices and their tendency to drag men down to the depths of the sea. There are just so many qualities to admire about these creatures. To honor their myriad achievements, let's enjoy some chilaquiles positively drowned in salsa.

Yield: 4 servings | Prep time: 10 minutes | Cook time: 20 minutes

1 (28-ounce) can whole peeled tomatoes, drained

½ medium onion, chopped

2 cloves garlic, minced

1 jalapeño, seeded and chopped

1 teaspoon ground cumin

salt and pepper, to taste

¼ cup vegetable oil

12 corn tortillas, cut into strips

½ cup crumbled cotija cheese, for serving

½ medium onion, chopped, for serving

¼ cup chopped fresh cilantro, for serving

1. In a blender, combine the drained tomatoes, chopped onion, garlic, jalapeño, cumin, salt, and pepper. Blend until smooth.

2. Heat the vegetable oil in a large skillet over medium-high heat. Add the tortilla strips and cook until crisp, stirring occasionally, about 5 minutes.

3. Pour the tomato mixture over the tortilla strips and cook for an additional 5 minutes, stirring occasionally.

4. Serve the chilaquiles topped with crumbled cotija cheese, chopped onion, and chopped cilantro.

BERMUDA LOVE TRIANGLE NACHOS

Stuck in a love triangle between two young, handsome monsters? Does it seem like an unending vortex of emotions? How tiresome. You deserve a break. Snack on these delicious chicken nachos as a form of self-care. The boys can wait. Nachos are your priority. Serve with Gothic Guacamole (page 40).

Yield: 4 servings | Prep time: 15 minutes | Cook time: 16 to 20 minutes

1 tablespoon olive oil

1 pound boneless, skinless chicken breasts, diced

1 teaspoon chili powder

½ teaspoon ground cumin

½ teaspoon garlic powder

½ teaspoon onion powder

½ teaspoon salt

¼ teaspoon pepper

¼ teaspoon paprika

¼ teaspoon cayenne pepper

1 serrano pepper, seeded and minced

½ cup sour cream

8 ounces tortilla chips

1 cup shredded cheddar cheese

½ cup chopped avocado, for serving

¼ cup chopped fresh cilantro, for serving

1. Preheat the oven to 375°F.

2. Heat the olive oil in a large skillet over medium-high heat. Add the chicken and cook until browned and cooked through, about 6 to 8 minutes.

3. Add the chili powder, cumin, garlic powder, onion powder, salt, pepper, paprika, and cayenne pepper to the skillet and stir to combine. Add the minced serrano pepper and stir again.

4. Reduce the heat to low and add the sour cream to the skillet. Stir until the sour cream is heated through and well combined with the chicken mixture.

5. Arrange the tortilla chips in a single layer on a baking sheet. Spoon the chicken mixture over the chips. Sprinkle the shredded cheddar cheese over the top of the chicken mixture.

6. Bake in the oven until the cheese is melted and bubbly, about 10 to 12 minutes.

7. Remove from the oven and sprinkle with chopped avocado and fresh cilantro.

THE PUR-LOINED LETTER

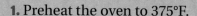

Edgar Allan Poe's stories involving his analytical detective C. Auguste Dupin are considered some of the first detective stories in literature. You've used some of his reasoning skills yourself while solving many crimes. To honor this trailblazing detective, make this flavorful pork loin.

Yield: 4 to 6 servings | Prep time: 15 minutes | Cook time: 1 hour, 15 minutes

1 (2-pound) pork loin

4 cloves garlic, minced

1 tablespoon fresh rosemary, chopped

2 tablespoons olive oil

4 large potatoes, cut into wedges

1 tablespoon paprika

½ teaspoon garlic powder

salt and pepper, to taste

1. Preheat the oven to 375°F.

2. Season the pork loin generously with salt and pepper, then rub it all over with minced garlic and chopped rosemary. Let it sit at room temperature for 15 minutes.

3. Heat the olive oil in a large oven-safe skillet over medium-high heat. Add the pork loin and sear on all sides until golden brown, about 3 to 4 minutes per side.

4. Transfer the skillet to the oven and roast for 45 to 50 minutes, or until the internal temperature of the pork reaches 145°F. Remove from the oven and let the pork rest for 10 minutes before slicing.

5. While the pork is roasting, prepare the potato wedges. In a large bowl, toss the potatoes with paprika, garlic powder, salt, and pepper.

6. Arrange the potato wedges on a baking sheet and bake in the oven for 30 to 35 minutes, or until crispy and golden brown.

7. Serve the sliced pork loin with the baked potato wedges on the side.

THE UNOFFICIAL WEDNESDAY COOKBOOK

SUGAR HELPS THE MEDICINE WOE DOWN

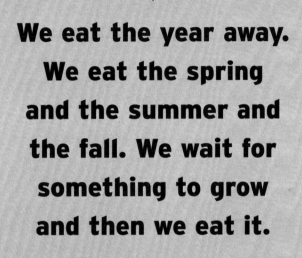

We eat the year away. We eat the spring and the summer and the fall. We wait for something to grow and then we eat it.

−Shirley Jackson,
We Have Always Lived in the Castle

QUAD ESPRESSO MILKSHAKE

Up late trying to figure out who framed your father for murder? Or writing the next great gothic masterpiece to make Shelley turn over in her grave? Leave drip coffee behind. This sweet treat packs a punch that will energize you through those tough hurdles and leave your enemies in the dust.

Yield: 1 milkshake | Prep time: 5 minutes

1 shot espresso (or ¼ cup strong coffee)

2 cups vanilla ice cream

½ cup whole milk

1 tablespoon chocolate syrup

whipped cream (optional)

1. Brew 1 shot of espresso or ¼ cup of strong coffee and let it cool to room temperature.

2. Add the ice cream, milk, and cooled espresso to a blender and blend until smooth.

3. Pour the milkshake into a glass. If using, top the milkshake with the whipped cream then drizzle the chocolate syrup on top.

WORD TO THE WOEFUL

We love a strong flavor. To increase the coffee flavor, add an extra shot (or three) of espresso. After all, you want your life to have purpose and meaning, right? To change the consistency of the milkshake, adjust the amount of milk.

COLORLESS COOKIES

Are you allergic to color? Does it make you break out in a rash and your skin peel off your bones? Well these colorless cookies may look half dead but they are fully delicious. Perfect for when you need a snack after redecorating your half of the room in your favorite colors: black and white.

Yield: 18 to 20 cookies | Prep time: 30 minutes, plus 1 hour to set | Cook time: 15 to 18 minutes

FOR THE COOKIES

2½ cups all-purpose flour

1 teaspoon baking powder

½ teaspoon baking soda

½ teaspoon salt

1¼ cups granulated sugar

1 cup unsalted butter, at room temperature

2 large eggs

1 teaspoon vanilla extract

½ cup whole milk

FOR THE FROSTING

2 cups powdered sugar

2 tablespoons light corn syrup

2 teaspoons fresh lemon juice

¼ teaspoon vanilla extract

2 to 3 tablespoons water

½ cup unsweetened cocoa powder

1. Preheat the oven to 350°F and line 2 baking sheets with parchment paper.

2. In a medium bowl, whisk together the flour, baking powder, baking soda, and salt. Set aside.

3. In a large bowl, beat the sugar and butter together until light and fluffy. Add the eggs, one at a time, beating well after each addition. Add the vanilla extract and beat until well combined.

4. Gradually add the dry ingredients to the wet mixture, alternating with the milk, and beating well after each addition.

5. Using a cookie scoop or tablespoon, drop the dough onto the prepared baking sheets, spacing them about 2 inches apart.

6. Bake for 15 to 18 minutes, or until the edges are lightly golden brown. Allow the cookies to cool completely on the baking sheets.

7. To make the frosting, whisk together the powdered sugar, corn syrup, lemon juice, vanilla extract, and enough water to make a smooth, thick glaze.

8. Divide the frosting in half. In one half, whisk in the cocoa powder to make the chocolate frosting. You may need to add more water at this step—add a little at a time until you achieve the desired consistency.

9. Using a small offset spatula or knife, spread the vanilla frosting on one half of each cookie, and the chocolate frosting on the other half.

10. Allow the frosting to set at room temperature for about an hour, or until firm.

HUMMER HONEY BANANA BREAD

Are you ready to feel the sting? Then suit up in your beekeeper's gear and harvest some fresh nectar … or just buy some local honey at the farmer's market. This banana bread uses the hard work of your fellow hummers (the bees obviously) to elevate this classic dessert into something you can serve your hive with pride. We like this best served warm with a favorite topping—add butter, cream cheese, or even a drizzle of honey on top.

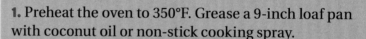

Yield: 1 loaf | Prep time: 10 minutes | Cook time: 50 to 60 minutes

2 ripe bananas
¼ cup milk
¼ cup honey
¼ cup melted coconut oil
2 eggs
1 teaspoon vanilla extract
1½ cups flour
1 teaspoon baking soda
½ teaspoon salt
½ cup shredded coconut

1. Preheat the oven to 350°F. Grease a 9-inch loaf pan with coconut oil or non-stick cooking spray.

2. In a large mixing bowl, mash the bananas with a fork. Add the milk, honey, melted coconut oil, eggs, and vanilla extract, and whisk until well combined.

3. In a separate bowl, mix together the flour, baking soda, and salt.

4. Add the dry ingredients to the wet ingredients and mix until just combined. Do not overmix.

5. Fold in the shredded coconut.

6. Pour the batter into the prepared loaf pan and bake for 50 to 60 minutes, or until a toothpick inserted into the center comes out clean.

7. Let the bread cool in the pan for 10 minutes, then remove it from the pan and transfer it to a wire rack to cool completely.

WORD TO THE WOEFUL

Want to experiment with flavor? The addition of the coconut in this recipe gives a nice texture and tropical flavor to the bread. For a deviously delicious flavor, add some chopped nuts or chocolate chips.

CHOCOLATE FUDGE

If you want the "authentic" fudge from an olde fudgery without stuffing free samples in your pockets, you must make this delicious recipe. Although fudge wasn't invented for years after the pilgrims arrived in the US, this fudge will have you pulling out your buckled hat nonetheless. Try sharing it with your friends and not hoarding it all for yourself—unless you have a spare pilgrim outfit to change into...

Yield: 16 to 20 small squares of fudge | Prep time: 5 minutes | Cook time: 2 minutes (microwaving) + 2 hours (refrigerating)

2 cups semisweet chocolate chips

1 (14-ounce) can sweetened condensed milk

1 teaspoon vanilla extract

1. Line an 8-inch square baking dish with parchment paper.

2. In a large microwave-safe bowl, combine the chocolate chips and sweetened condensed milk.

3. Microwave on high for 1 minute, then stir. Continue microwaving in 30-second intervals, stirring after each, until the chocolate is completely melted and smooth, about 1 minute more.

4. Stir in the vanilla extract.

5. Pour the fudge mixture into the prepared baking dish and spread it out evenly.

6. Refrigerate for at least 2 hours, or until the fudge is firm.

7. Once the fudge is firm, remove it from the pan using the parchment paper and cut it into small squares.

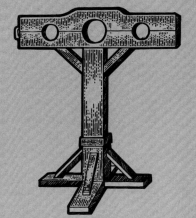

WORD TO THE WOEFUL

Creativity is the heart of baking. Be sure to add nuts, dried fruits, or any other ingredients you like. If you prefer the darkness of the void, use dark chocolate instead of semisweet. If you're making this for your super-sweet roommate, milk chocolate works as well.

BLACK CAT BROWNIES

Poe's "The Black Cat" as the mascot for a team? That sounds purr-fect! What better motivator than a cautionary tale of alcoholism, guilt, and murder? These delectable chocolate treats may not be strong enough to wall your latest victim in, but they are good enough to eat.

Yield: 12 brownies | Prep time: 15 minutes | Cook time: 25 to 30 minutes

1 cup (2 sticks) unsalted butter

2¼ cups granulated sugar

4 large eggs

1¼ cups unsweetened cocoa powder

1 teaspoon salt

1 teaspoon baking powder

1 teaspoon espresso powder (optional)

1 tablespoon vanilla extract

1½ cups all-purpose flour

2 cups dark chocolate chips

1. Preheat the oven to 350°F. Grease a 9 x 13-inch baking pan.

2. Melt the butter in a saucepan or in the microwave. Add the sugar and stir until well combined.

3. In a separate bowl, whisk the eggs together. Add the cocoa powder, salt, baking powder, espresso powder (if using), and vanilla extract. Whisk until well combined.

4. Add the melted butter and sugar mixture to the bowl with the egg mixture. Whisk until well combined.

5. Fold in the flour and dark chocolate chips until just combined.

6. Pour the batter into the prepared baking pan and spread it out evenly.

7. Bake for 25 to 30 minutes, or until a toothpick inserted into the center comes out clean.

8. Let the brownies cool in the pan for at least 10 minutes before slicing and serving.

WORD TO THE WOEFUL

Although you are the toughest of young crime solvers, we don't want our brownies to be. Be sure not to overmix the batter or the brownies may become tough.

THE UNOFFICIAL WEDNESDAY COOKBOOK

UNICORN CUPCAKE

Hypothetically, if you had to do something nice for your roommate/maybe best friend outside of lending a sentient hand, maybe you would make some treats using their favorite colors. If so, you should probably just use all the colors out there, just guessing based on said person's decorating habits. These cupcakes would be a safe bet then! They are colorful to say the least.

Yield: 12 cupcakes | Prep time: 20 minutes | Cook time: 18 to 20 minutes

FOR THE CUPCAKES
1½ cups all-purpose flour

1 teaspoon baking powder

¼ teaspoon baking soda

¼ teaspoon salt

½ cup unsalted butter, at room temperature

1 cup granulated sugar

2 large eggs, at room temperature

2 teaspoons vanilla extract

½ cup whole milk

½ cup rainbow sprinkles

FOR THE FROSTING
1 cup unsalted butter, at room temperature

4 cups powdered sugar

¼ cup heavy cream

2 teaspoons vanilla extract

pinch of salt

assorted food coloring

1. Preheat the oven to 350°F and line a muffin tin with cupcake liners.

2. In a medium mixing bowl, whisk together the flour, baking powder, baking soda, and salt. Set aside.

3. In a separate large mixing bowl, cream the butter and sugar together until light and fluffy.

4. Add the eggs one at a time, mixing well after each addition, then stir in the vanilla extract.

5. Gradually add the dry ingredients to the wet mixture in three parts, alternating with the milk. Mix until just combined.

6. Fold in the rainbow sprinkles.

7. Scoop the batter into the cupcake liners until they are about three quarters full.

8. Bake for 18 to 20 minutes, or until a toothpick inserted in the center of a cupcake comes out clean.

9. Remove the cupcakes from the oven and let them cool in the muffin tin for 5 minutes before transferring them to a wire rack to cool completely.

10. While the cupcakes are cooling, prepare the frosting. In a large mixing bowl, beat the butter until light and creamy. Gradually add the powdered sugar, alternating with the heavy cream. Mix in the vanilla extract and salt.

11. Divide the frosting into separate bowls and add a different food coloring to each one, creating pastel shades.

12. Once the cupcakes are completely cooled, pipe the frosting onto each cupcake using a piping bag or a ziplock bag with the corner snipped off.

13. Top each cupcake with additional rainbow sprinkles, if desired.

WORD TO THE WOEFUL

We know you're not familiar with pastels, so allow us to give you some tips. To create these shades, start with a small amount of food coloring and gradually add more until you've created the desired color.

Ice Crystal Candy

Lace up your dancing shoes and get ready to party, but only as a cover for an ongoing investigation. Nevermore's annual dance might be the year's biggest event, but you've got more important things going on, so why not fuel up on some thematically appropriate icy crystal candy? It has the sugar rush that all good detectives need to find clues, become a dancing sensation, and get covered in fake blood.

Yield: 12 to 15 rock candy sticks | Prep time: 15 minutes | Cook time: 10 to 14 days

1 cup water

2 cups granulated sugar

food coloring (optional)

flavor extract (optional)

wooden skewers or
candy sticks

clothespins or binder clips

medium saucepan

1. Bring the water to a boil in a medium saucepan.

2. Gradually add the sugar, stirring constantly until it dissolves.

3. Remove the saucepan from the heat and let the syrup cool slightly.

4. If using food coloring or flavor extract, stir it into the syrup.

5. Dip the wooden skewers or candy sticks into the syrup.

6. Secure the skewers to the top of the saucepan with clothespins or binder clips, making sure they don't touch the bottom or sides of the pan.

7. Let the syrup cool and evaporate for 10 to 14 days, until sugar crystals have formed and grown to the desired size.

8. Once the rock candy has formed, remove the skewers from the saucepan and enjoy!

WORD TO THE WOEFUL

This is another chance to be a mad scientist. Experiment with different flavors and colors by adding extract and food coloring to the syrup before it cools. Don't you feel like you're creating a horrific creature that may take form and seek revenge against you? How wonderful. But be patient! Rock candy takes a while to form, so don't be tempted to check on it too often. We can't disturb it while it's growing—ghastly things take time.

POTPOURRI "CANDY"

Dried flowers and fruits have never been considered a mainstream culinary delicacy but to certain male members of the family, nothing has been as enticing as a bowl of potpourri, especially in times of stress. These candy interpolations of the classic scented room accessories will be far more crowd-pleasing and way more digestible. You can still leave a bowl of the original out for any brothers who may be gluttons for punishment.

Yield: Around 20 candy pieces | Prep time: 20 minutes | Cook time: 1 hour

2 large navel oranges

2 cups granulated sugar

1 cup water

6 ounces semisweet chocolate chips

1 tablespoon vegetable shortening

flaky salt, to taste

1. Cut the ends off each orange then slice them thinly into rounds approximately ⅛ inch thick.

2. In a large saucepan, combine the sugar and water and heat over medium heat, stirring occasionally, until the sugar dissolves completely.

3. Add the orange slices to the sugar syrup and bring to a simmer. Reduce the heat to low and cook the oranges for 45 to 60 minutes, until they become translucent and the syrup has thickened.

4. Remove the orange slices from the syrup and place them on a wire rack to dry for a few hours, or overnight.

5. Melt the chocolate chips and shortening in a double boiler or microwave, stirring until smooth.

6. Dip the bottom half of each orange slice in the melted chocolate and place them on a sheet of parchment paper to dry. Sprinkle with flaky salt.

7. Let the slices dry completely before serving or storing in an airtight container.

A birthday is one of the most dreadful occasions. The body creeping closer to death's door. Time's hand slowly ushering us toward our twilight years. Truly wonderful. What better way to celebrate than with a cake as dark and macabre as the day's mood?

Yield: 12 to 16 servings | Prep time: 30 minutes, plus 20 to 30 minutes to set | Cook time: 30 to 35 minutes per cake layer

2 cups all-purpose flour

¾ cup unsweetened cocoa powder

2 cups granulated sugar

2 teaspoons baking powder

1½ teaspoons baking soda

1 teaspoon salt

1 cup milk

½ cup vegetable oil

2 eggs

2 teaspoons vanilla extract

1 cup boiling water

2 cups heavy cream

¼ cup unsalted butter

16 ounces dark chocolate chips or chopped chocolate

1. Preheat the oven to 350°F. Grease and flour three 9-inch round cake pans. Cut out three parchment paper rounds to fit at the bottom of each cake pan and place in each.

2. In a large mixing bowl, whisk together the flour, cocoa powder, sugar, baking powder, baking soda, and salt.

3. Add the milk, vegetable oil, eggs, and vanilla extract and beat on medium speed until well combined.

4. Add boiling water and mix until the batter is smooth.

5. Pour the batter evenly into the prepared pans. Bake for 30 to 35 minutes, or until a toothpick inserted in the center of the cake comes out clean.

6. Remove the cakes from the oven and allow them to cool completely on a wire rack.

7. In a saucepan, heat the heavy cream and unsalted butter over medium heat until the butter has melted and the cream is hot but not boiling.

8. Remove the saucepan from the heat and add the dark chocolate chips/chopped chocolate. Let the mixture sit for 5 minutes, then whisk until smooth.

9. Chill the chocolate ganache in the refrigerator for 20 to 30 minutes or until it has thickened and is spreadable.

9. Chill the chocolate ganache in the refrigerator for 20 to 30 minutes or until it has thickened and is spreadable.

10. Assemble the cake by spreading a layer of ganache frosting between each cake layer and on top of the cake.

11. Decorate the cake with additional chocolate shavings or sprinkles, if desired.

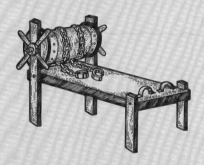

WORD TO THE WOEFUL

Messy is hardly one of Wednesday's qualities. Allow cake layers to cool completely before frosting, or the frosting may melt and slide off. If you want a deeper, richer chocolate flavor, use high-quality cocoa powder and dark chocolate chips/chopped chocolate. Chill the cake in the refrigerator for 30 minutes to an hour before serving to allow the frosting to set. While you're waiting, perhaps it's time to break out the spider piñata.

Piñata Peanut Butter Spider Cookies

At a child's birthday, you want to ensure the perfect cake, and just as important—the perfect party game. A piñata is a time-honored tradition, sure to bring shrieks of joy and, in the Addams's case, fear. Wednesday's piñata was filled with spiders instead of candy, and these creepy cookies honor the birthday girl. Feliz cumpleaños, Wednesday.

Yield: 24 cookies | Prep time: 20 minutes | Cook time: 10 to 12 minutes

1¼ cups all-purpose flour
½ teaspoon baking powder
½ teaspoon baking soda
¼ teaspoon salt
½ cup unsalted butter, at room temperature
½ cup creamy peanut butter
½ cup granulated sugar
½ cup brown sugar
1 egg
1 teaspoon vanilla extract
¼ cup dark chocolate chips
24 Lindt Lindor Truffles (any flavor)
48 candy eyes

1. Preheat the oven to 350°F and line a baking sheet with parchment paper.

2. In a medium bowl, whisk together the flour, baking powder, baking soda, and salt. Set aside.

3. In a large mixing bowl, cream together the butter, peanut butter, granulated sugar, and brown sugar until light and fluffy, about 2 to 3 minutes.

4. Add in the egg and vanilla extract and mix until well combined.

5. Gradually stir in the dry ingredients until a smooth dough forms.

6. Roll the dough into 24 balls and place them 2 inches apart on the prepared baking sheet.

7. Flatten the balls slightly with the palm of your hand.

8. Bake for 10 to 12 minutes or until the edges are lightly golden brown.

9. Remove from the oven and make an indent with the back of a spoon to create a hole for the truffles.

10. Let cool for a few minutes on the baking sheet before transferring to a wire rack to cool completely.

11. Once the cookies have cooled, melt the chocolate chips in the microwave or in a double boiler.

12. Dot a small amount of chocolate into the hole of each cookie.

13. Place a Lindt Lindor Truffle on top of each cookie.

14. To decorate, attach two candy eyes onto each truffle with a small dab of chocolate. Pipe spider legs coming out from the truffle onto the cookie.

15. Make a small indent in each truffle to make a mouth.

WORD TO THE WOEFUL

If you don't have candy eyes, you can use mini chocolate chips or black icing dots instead. Actual spider eyes are not recommended—just so untidy.

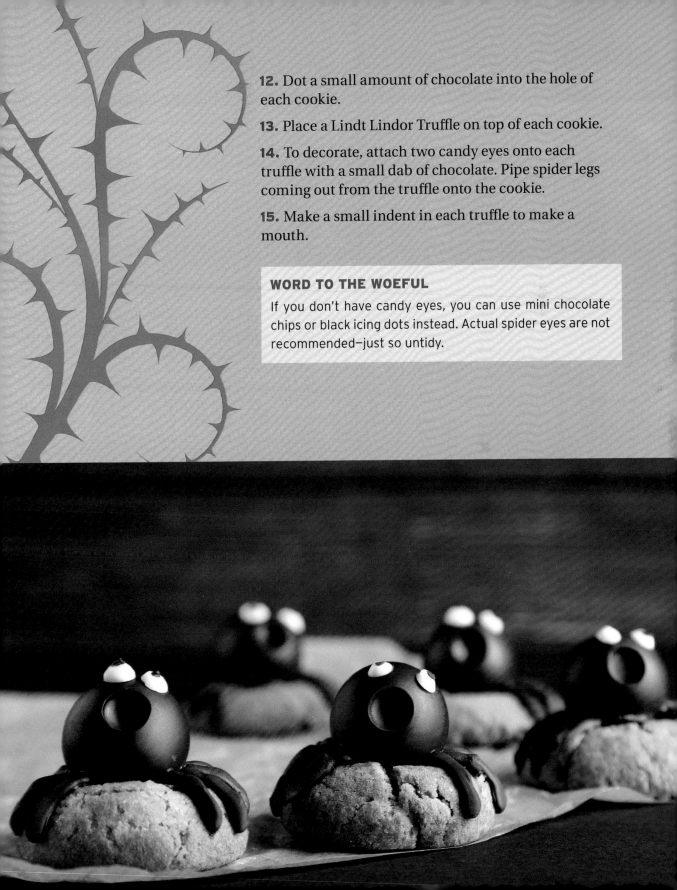

BLOOD ORANGE ICE POPS

Summer is not an ideal time for an Addams. There is just so much sunshine and giddy children running amok. If you need some time to yourself to cool down while not sacrificing taste, try these blood orange ice pops.

Yield: 6 ice pops | Prep time: 10 minutes | Cook time: 10 minutes, plus 6 hours to freeze

4 to 5 medium blood oranges
¼ cup granulated sugar
¼ cup water
¼ cup fresh lime juice

1. Cut the blood oranges in half and squeeze the juice into a bowl. Use a strainer to remove any seeds.

2. In a small saucepan, mix together the sugar and water. Heat over medium heat, stirring constantly, until the sugar is completely dissolved. Remove from the heat and let cool.

3. Mix the cooled sugar syrup, lime juice, and blood orange juice together.

4. Pour the mixture into ice pop molds, filling each mold about two thirds of the way full.

5. Freeze the popsicles for about 2 hours or until they are semifrozen.

6. Insert ice pop sticks into each mold and continue to freeze for another 4 hours, or until completely frozen.

7. To remove the ice pops, run the molds under warm water for a few seconds to loosen them.

WORD TO THE WOEFUL

If you don't have ice pop molds at the ready, use small paper cups and ice pop sticks instead. If blood oranges are not in season, you may make do with regular oranges instead. They may not be quite as spooky, but you bring the spookiness wherever you go.

PARENT WEEKEND S'MORES MOUSSE

Weekends with parents can occasionally be difficult. It can bring up a lot of things—complicated family dynamics, hidden emotions, or maybe a secret past murder. Ease the tension with a twist on a classic treat. There may be sticky situations, but together you can make it through anything.

Yield: 4 to 6 servings | Prep time: 20 minutes, plus 2 hours to set | Cook time: 10 minutes

1 cup heavy cream

1 cup milk chocolate chips

6 standard-size marshmallows, plus extra for topping

1 cup graham cracker crumbs (about 8 to 10 whole graham crackers)

4 tablespoons unsalted butter, melted

¼ teaspoon salt

whipped cream, for serving (optional)

1. In a medium saucepan, heat the heavy cream over medium heat until it begins to simmer.

2. Remove from heat and add in the milk chocolate chips and marshmallows. Stir until completely melted and smooth.

3. In a small bowl, combine the graham cracker crumbs, melted butter, and salt. Mix until well combined.

4. Divide the graham cracker mixture evenly among 6 serving dishes. Press down firmly to create a crust.

5. Pour the chocolate mixture on top of the graham cracker crust, dividing it evenly among the dishes.

6. Refrigerate the dishes for at least 2 hours, or until the mousse has set.

7. Once set, remove from the fridge and top with extra standard-size marshmallows.

8. Use a kitchen torch or broil in the oven for a few minutes to toast the marshmallows to your desired level of char.

9. Serve chilled, topped with whipped cream if desired.

CRIME STOPPER COBBLER

Not too far from Nevermore sits a beloved cafe and bakery that entices the entire town, including the local sheriff, the town's noble mayor, troubled teens, former locals who have faked their own deaths, and so many more. Included here is a delicious cobbler that may inspire you to solve a mystery and save the town.

Yield: 6 to 8 servings | Prep time: 15 minutes | Cook time: 35 to 40 minutes

4 cups fresh blueberries

½ cup granulated sugar, divided

1 tablespoon cornstarch

1 teaspoon vanilla extract

½ teaspoon ground cinnamon

¼ teaspoon ground nutmeg

1 cup all-purpose flour

¼ cup brown sugar

1½ teaspoons baking powder

½ teaspoon salt

6 tablespoons unsalted butter, chilled and cut into small pieces

¼ cup boiling water

1. Preheat the oven to 375°F. Grease an 8-inch square baking dish.

2. In a medium bowl, combine the blueberries, ¼ cup of granulated sugar, cornstarch, vanilla extract, cinnamon, and nutmeg. Mix well and pour the mixture into the prepared baking dish.

3. In a large bowl, whisk together the flour, the remaining ¼ cup of granulated sugar, brown sugar, baking powder, and salt.

4. Cut in the chilled butter with a pastry blender or your fingertips until the mixture resembles coarse crumbs.

5. Stir in boiling water until just combined.

6. Drop spoonfuls at a time of the mixture over the blueberries in the baking dish.

7. Bake for 35 to 40 minutes or until the topping is golden brown and the blueberries are bubbling.

8. Let cool for a few minutes before serving.

WORD TO THE WOEFUL

Have the local bog witches used all the fresh blueberries? Frozen blueberries can be substituted. Make sure to thaw them and drain them off any excess liquid before using.

BLACK MOONS

Imagine: It's a dark night as you stroll through your favorite graveyard. The breeze tousles your braids and the dry leaves crunch under your black platform shoes. You're meeting your undead friends under the blackest of moons, and they're hungry. These delicious cookies would do their appetite justice.

Yield: 12 to 15 minutes | Prep time: 15 minutes | Cook time: 10 to 12 minutes

2 cups all-purpose flour

½ cup unsweetened cocoa powder

1½ teaspoons baking soda

½ teaspoon salt

½ cup vegetable shortening

1 cup granulated sugar

1 large egg

1 teaspoon vanilla extract

1 cup milk

FOR THE FILLING

½ cup unsalted butter, at room temperature

1 cup powdered sugar

1 cup marshmallow cream

½ teaspoon vanilla extract

1. Preheat the oven to 375°F. Line 2 baking sheets with parchment paper.

2. In a medium bowl, whisk together the flour, cocoa powder, baking soda, and salt.

3. In a large bowl, beat the shortening and sugar until light and fluffy. Add the egg and vanilla extract, and beat until well combined.

4. Gradually mix in the flour mixture and milk, alternating between the two until everything is combined.

5. Using a spoon or cookie scoop, drop spoonfuls of batter onto the prepared baking sheets, spacing them about 2 inches apart.

6. Bake for 10 to 12 minutes, until the edges are set and the tops spring back when lightly touched.

7. Allow the Black Moons to cool on the baking sheets for a few minutes before transferring them to a wire rack to cool completely.

FOR THE FILLING

1. In a large bowl, beat the butter until creamy. Gradually add the powdered sugar, beating until light and fluffy.

2. Beat in the marshmallow cream and vanilla extract until well combined.

3. Once the Black Moons have cooled completely, spread the filling on the flat side of one pie and top with another pie to form a sandwich.

4. Serve immediately or store in an airtight container at room temperature for up to 3 days.

WORD TO THE WOEFUL

Feel like something softer than usual? For a cake-like texture, reduce the baking time by a minute or two. If you prefer a firmer texture, you can bake them for a few extra minutes.

Red Thumbprint Cookies

Some people are blessed with a green thumb and have the ability to grow and nurture beautiful, peaceful plants. Other people are cursed with a red thumb and care for the world's more frightening and carnivorous plants. These cookies are a nod to our preference.

Yield: 20 to 24 cookies | Prep time: 15 to 20 minutes | Cook time: 12 to 15 minutes

1 cup unsalted butter, softened

2/3 cup granulated sugar

½ teaspoon vanilla extract

2¼ cups all-purpose flour

¼ teaspoon salt

½ cup strawberry jam

1. Preheat the oven to 350°F.

2. In a large mixing bowl, cream the softened butter, granulated sugar, and vanilla extract until light and fluffy.

3. In a separate bowl, sift together the all-purpose flour and salt. Gradually add this to the butter mixture, mixing until just combined.

4. Roll the dough into 1½-inch balls and place them onto a baking sheet lined with parchment paper. Use your thumb or the back of a spoon to create an indentation in the center of each cookie.

5. Spoon a small amount (about ½ teaspoon) of strawberry jam into each indentation.

6. Bake the cookies for 12 to 15 minutes, or until they're lightly golden brown around the edges.

7. Remove the cookies from the oven and let them cool on the baking sheet for a few minutes before transferring them to a wire rack to cool completely.

Real Girl Scout Cookies

Perky little girls who believe in the power of teamwork and friendship. It can be ... a lot for some of the more macabre children in the neighborhood. If perhaps they are searching for cookies made from real Girl Scouts, try consoling them with these handmade shortbread treats.

Yield: 24 cookies | Prep time: 15 to 20 minutes, plus 30 to 60 minutes to chill | Cook time: 25 to 30 minutes

2 cups all-purpose flour

¼ teaspoon salt

1 cup unsalted butter,
at room temperature

½ cup sugar

1 teaspoon vanilla extract

coarse sugar, for
sprinkling (optional)

1. Preheat the oven to 350°F and line an 8 x 8-inch baking dish with parchment paper.

2. In a medium bowl, whisk together the flour and salt.

3. In a large mixing bowl, cream the butter and sugar until light and fluffy, about 3 to 4 minutes.

4. Add the vanilla extract to the butter mixture and mix well.

5. Gradually add in the flour mixture to the butter mixture and mix until the dough comes together.

6. Press the dough into the prepared baking dish and smooth the surface with a spatula or the back of a spoon. Chill for 30 minutes to an hour.

7. Use a knife or a pizza cutter to cut the dough into 24 fingers, then prick the surface with a fork.

8. If desired, sprinkle coarse sugar over the top of the shortbread fingers.

9. Bake for 25 to 30 minutes, or until the edges are lightly golden.

10. Remove from the oven and allow the shortbread fingers to cool completely in the baking dish.

11. Once cooled, remove the shortbread fingers from the dish and serve.

WORD TO THE WOEFUL

Take care, gothic friends! Overworking the dough or the shortbread will cause it to become tough. Another quick hint? Using a pizza cutter to cut the shortbread fingers makes it easier to get clean, straight edges. Plus, it feels so satisfying to slice those fingers.

"Secret" Ginger Snaps

The hidden room of Nevermore's secret society requires a peculiar cracking sound to reveal itself. **S**eems **N**ot **A** **P**articularly **T**ight **W**ay of **I**ncreasing **C**oncealment from **E**nemies, but we do love the way it harkens back to our favorite theme song. Can't you hear it now?

Yield: About 30 cookies | Prep time: 15 to 20 minutes | Cook time: 10 to 12 minutes

2¼ cups all-purpose flour

2 teaspoons ground ginger

1 teaspoon baking soda

½ teaspoon ground cinnamon

½ teaspoon ground cloves

¼ teaspoon salt

¾ cup unsalted butter, at room temperature

1 cup granulated sugar, plus more for rolling

1 large egg

¼ cup molasses

1. Preheat the oven to 350°F. Line a baking sheet with parchment paper.

2. In a medium bowl, whisk together the flour, ginger, baking soda, cinnamon, cloves, and salt.

3. In a large mixing bowl, cream the butter and sugar until light and fluffy, about 3 to 4 minutes.

4. Add the egg and molasses to the butter mixture and mix well.

5. Gradually add in the flour mixture to the butter mixture and mix until the dough comes together.

6. Roll the dough into 1-inch balls, then roll the balls in granulated sugar to coat.

7. Place the balls 2 inches apart on the prepared baking sheet.

8. Bake for 10 to 12 minutes, or until the edges are firm and the centers are slightly soft.

9. Remove from the oven and allow the cookies to cool on the baking sheet for 5 minutes, then transfer to a wire rack to cool completely.

10. Store the cookies in an airtight container at room temperature for up to 1 week.

THE UNOFFICIAL WEDNESDAY COOKBOOK

MARIE'S RED VELVET CAKE

Let them eat cake! Across several versions of the Addams family, Wednesday practices her guillotine skills on her beloved doll Marie Antoinette. Enjoy some blood-red cake with your own headless doll, perhaps while discussing various revolutions you're planning.

Yield: 12 to 16 servings | Prep time: 30 minutes | Cook time: 30 to 35 minutes

2½ cups all-purpose flour

1½ cups granulated sugar

1 teaspoon baking soda

1 teaspoon salt

1 teaspoon cocoa powder

1½ cups vegetable oil

1 cup buttermilk

2 large eggs

1 tablespoon red food coloring

1 teaspoon vanilla extract

1 tablespoon white vinegar

1 batch cream cheese frosting (recipe below)

½ cup red velvet cake crumbs

FOR THE CREAM CHEESE FROSTING

16 ounces cream cheese, softened

1 cup unsalted butter, softened

6 cups powdered sugar

1 teaspoon vanilla extract

1. Preheat the oven to 350°F and grease three 8-inch cake pans.

2. In a large mixing bowl, whisk together the flour, sugar, baking soda, salt, and cocoa powder.

3. In a separate mixing bowl, mix together the vegetable oil, buttermilk, eggs, red food coloring, vanilla extract, and white vinegar.

4. Gradually mix the wet ingredients into the dry ingredients, stirring until just combined.

5. Divide the batter evenly between the 3 prepared cake pans.

6. Bake for 30 to 35 minutes or until a toothpick inserted into the center of the cake comes out clean.

7. Allow the cakes to cool in the pans for 10 minutes before removing them from the pans and placing them on a wire rack to cool completely.

8. Once the cakes are cool, prepare the cream cheese frosting by beating the cream cheese and butter together until light and fluffy. Gradually beat in the powdered sugar and vanilla extract until the frosting is smooth.

9. To assemble the cake, place 1 cake layer on a cake stand or plate and spread a layer of frosting on top. Repeat with the remaining layers, spreading frosting between each layer.

10. Use the remaining frosting to frost the top and sides of the cake.

11. Crush the red velvet cake crumbs and sprinkle them on top of the cake.

WORD TO THE WOEFUL

Want to get your hands messy, perhaps filled with red mush? You're in luck! To make the red velvet cake crumbs, crumble up some leftover red velvet cake or make a small cake specifically for this purpose.

"Poison" Caramel Apples

Have a princess you need to remove from a situation? There's no harm in borrowing from a classic. Try these delicious caramel apples—no actual poison, but the princess will be distracted by the sticky sweet treat.

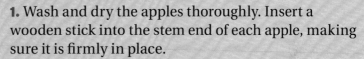

Yield: 6 candy apples | Prep time: 10 minutes | Cook time: 20 minutes

6 medium apples
2 cups granulated sugar
¾ cups water
½ cup light corn syrup
red food coloring
candy thermometer

1. Wash and dry the apples thoroughly. Insert a wooden stick into the stem end of each apple, making sure it is firmly in place.

2. Line a baking sheet with parchment paper and set aside.

3. In a medium saucepan, combine the sugar, water, and corn syrup. Cook over medium heat, stirring constantly, until the sugar dissolves.

4. Insert the candy thermometer into the mixture and bring it to a boil. Let it boil until it reaches 300°F, also known as the "hard crack" stage.

5. Remove the mixture from the heat and stir in a few drops of red food coloring until you achieve the desired color.

6. Working quickly, dip each apple into the candy mixture, making sure to coat it completely. Allow any excess candy mixture to drip off before placing the apple onto the prepared baking sheet.

7. Repeat with the remaining apples and let them cool at room temperature until the candy coating is hard and shiny.

WORD TO THE WOEFUL
Choose spookier wooden sticks, ideally gnarled branches, to give your own gothic twist.

MERINGUE GHOSTS

Occasionally, a ghost may appear in the Addams family mansion. They're terrible, frightening, and invasive. You may miss them while at Nevermore. Create some of these meringue ghosts to keep you company—or just when you need a little snack.

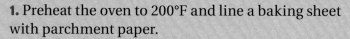

Yield: 12 to 15 ghosts | Prep time: 15 minutes | Cook time: 2 hours

3 egg whites, at room temperature

½ teaspoon cream of tartar

¾ cup granulated sugar

½ teaspoon vanilla extract

mini chocolate chips or black frosting, for the eyes

1. Preheat the oven to 200°F and line a baking sheet with parchment paper.

2. In a large mixing bowl, beat the egg whites with an electric mixer on medium speed until they become frothy.

3. Add the cream of tartar and continue beating until soft peaks form.

4. Gradually add in the sugar while continuing to beat on high speed until stiff peaks form and the meringue is glossy and thick.

5. Add in the vanilla extract and mix until just combined.

6. Transfer the meringue to a piping bag fitted with a round tip.

7. Pipe the meringue ghosts onto the prepared baking sheet, making sure to leave enough space between them.

8. Use mini chocolate chips or black frosting to create eyes for each ghost.

9. Bake the meringue ghosts for about 2 hours, or until they are dry and crispy to the touch.

10. Turn off the oven and let the meringue ghosts cool completely inside the oven with the door slightly open.

11. Once cooled, carefully remove the meringue ghosts from the parchment paper and serve immediately or store in an airtight container.

WORD TO THE WOEFUL

Ghosts can be difficult to correctly summon. Here are some conjuring tricks: When piping the ghosts, make sure to hold the piping bag directly above the baking sheet and gently squeeze until the meringue reaches the desired height. Then, stop squeezing and quickly pull the piping bag away to create a ghost-like shape.

WOE YOUR WHISTLE

**Double, double
toil and trouble;
Fire burn and
cauldron bubble.**

—William Shakespeare,
Macbeth

PIRANHA PUNCH

When it comes to family, an Addams pulls no punches. Piranhas, sword fights, conspiracy—all are tried and true methods to protect your family. After you seek your revenge against the pathetic interloper who threatened your family member, invite your entire clan to a party and serve this sweet drink.

Yield: 4 to 6 servings | Prep time: 5 minutes, plus 1 hour to chill

2 cups blue Hawaiian Punch

1 cup pineapple juice

¼ cup orange juice

¼ cup lime juice

½ cup lemon-lime soda (for nonalcoholic version) or vodka (for alcoholic version)

dried pineapple and rosemary sprigs, for garnishing

1. In a large pitcher, mix together the blue Hawaiian Punch, pineapple juice, orange juice, and lime juice.

2. If making the non-alcohoic version, add in the lemon-lime soda. If making the alcoholic version, add in the vodka.

3. Stir until all ingredients are well combined.

4. Chill the mixture in the refrigerator for at least an hour before serving.

5. To serve, fill a glass with ice cubes and pour the blue punch over it.

6. Garnish with dried pineapple and a sprig of rosemary.

WORD TO THE WOEFUL

If you for some reason require a sweeter version, add a bit of honey or sugar to taste.

Dark Side Dahlia

Everyone has a dark side within. Luckily for Wednesday, she's mostly dark side. To indulge the dark and light within you, try this delicious drink. With the addition of the cherry, it is a perfect balance of sweet and bitter. Perhaps you can invite your overly sweet roommate to join you. A little bit of both makes for a good team.

Yield: 1 cocktail | Prep time: 5 minutes

2 ounces gin

¾ ounce Barolo Chinato

3 dashes Angostura bitters

maraschino cherry,
for garnish

1. Pour the gin, Barolo Chinato, bitters, and ice into a mixing glass, and stir until the liquid is chilled.

2. Strain the mixture into a martini glass.

3. Garnish the rim with the maraschino cherry and serve.

WORD TO THE WOEFUL

The Black Dahlia is one of the most notorious unsolved murders in the United States. Take a drink in honor of its victim, Elizabeth Short, while you tackle your own unsolved crimes.

NIGHTSHADE NEGRONI

Deadly nightshade is a commonly known poison. Equally dangerous is Nevermore Academy's secret society. Though Wednesday herself finds the club a little trivial, it is good to know a drink recipe to enjoy in the hidden library.

Yield: 1 drink | Prep time: 5 minutes

1 ounce gin

1 ounce sweet vermouth

1 ounce Campari

orange peel or orange wedge, for garnish

1. Fill a rocks glass with ice.

2. Add equal parts gin, sweet vermouth, and Campari to the glass.

3. Stir gently until the cocktail is well chilled.

4. Strain the cocktail into a new rocks glass filled with fresh ice.

5. Garnish with a strip of orange peel or an orange wedge.

WORD TO THE WOEFUL

Addamses like a very bitter drink. But if you or a guest find the drink too bitter, adjust the ratio of ingredients to your liking, such as adding a bit more sweet vermouth or gin.

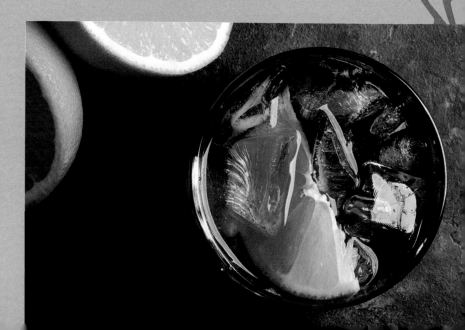

NEVERMORE NIGHTCAP

It's been a long day of solving mysteries, escaping monsters, and confronting murderous teachers. It's finally time to unwind with your favorite sounds of wails and rattling chains. Pair this soothing soundtrack with a relaxing nightcap.

Yield: 1 cocktail | Prep time: 5 minutes

2 ounces gin

1 ounce blue curaçao

1 ounce cranberry juice

1 ounce pineapple juice

½ ounce lemon juice

½ ounce simple syrup

edible flower, for garnish (optional)

1. Fill a shaker with ice.

2. Add the gin, blue curaçao, cranberry juice, pineapple juice, lemon juice, and simple syrup.

3. Shake well to combine.

4. Strain into a chilled glass.

5. Garnish with an edible flower, if desired.

WORD TO THE WOEFUL

We prefer the aggressive shaking of a cocktail shaker to relieve some tension. However, if you don't have a shaker, it works to stir the ingredients in a glass with ice.

OPHELIA OLD FASHIONED

One of the great halls of Nevermore is named after this tragic Shakespearean heroine. While we don't recommend drowning your sorrows, we do recommend staring tragically out of rain-splattered windows while responsibly sipping this drink. An occasional dip into the depressive can be good for the soul, but don't forget the bright side—there is always rage to try feeling next.

Yield: 1 cocktail | Prep time: 5 minutes

1 teaspoon simple syrup
or 1 sugar cube

2 dashes Angostura bitters

2 ounces bourbon
or rye whiskey

1 orange twist, for garnishing

1 brandied cherry,
for garnishing

1. In a rocks glass, muddle the simple syrup (or sugar cube) and bitters together until the sugar is dissolved.

2. Add ice cubes to the glass and pour in the bourbon or rye whiskey.

3. Stir the mixture for about 30 seconds to chill and dilute the drink slightly.

4. Garnish with the orange twist and brandied cherry.

WORD TO THE WOEFUL

A brandied cherry is wickedly easy to make. Just combine 1 cup of pitted cherries, ½ cup of brandy, and ½ cup of granulated sugar in a small saucepan. Cook over medium heat until the sugar dissolves and the mixture thickens slightly. Let cool before using as a garnish. Store any leftover brandied cherries in an airtight container in the fridge for up to 1 week.

BLOODY MARY

Ready to toast to a powerful woman? Whip this classic cocktail up one evening and look in the mirror. You can toast to yourself, of course, or you can say this cocktail's name to the mirror three times. See what happens—either way you'll be face to face with a terrifying creature.

Yield: 1 drink | Prep time: 5 minutes

1½ ounces vodka (omit for nonalcoholic version)

4 ounces tomato juice

½ ounce lemon juice

½ ounce Worcestershire sauce

¼ teaspoon hot sauce (add more for a spicier drink)

¼ teaspoon celery salt

¼ teaspoon pepper

celery stalk, olives, pickles, lemon wedge, and cooked bacon, for garnishing (optional)

1. If making the alcoholic version, pour the vodka into a highball glass filled with ice.

2. Add the tomato juice, lemon juice, Worcestershire sauce, hot sauce, celery salt, and pepper.

3. Stir well to combine.

4. Taste and adjust seasonings as needed.

5. Garnish with a celery stalk, olives, pickles, a lemon wedge, and/or cooked bacon, if desired.

WORD TO THE WOEFUL

Want a version without alcohol? Simply omit the vodka and add a splash of water or extra tomato juice to make up for the lost liquid. If you want more spice in order to feel the burn, muddle a few slices of jalapeño or serrano pepper in the glass before adding other ingredients.

YETI MARTINI

Nevermore is home to a wide variety of outcasts, including the now extinct Yeti. One of the best ways to honor the monsters of the past is to indulge in the sweet taste of an ironic cocktail. Take a sip, think of monsters, and enjoy.

Yield: 1 serving | Prep time: 5 minutes

2 ounces vodka or 2 ounces lemon-lime soda for nonalcoholic version

1 ounce blue curaçao or blue curaçao syrup for a nonalcoholic version

1 ounce pineapple juice

1 ounce sweet and sour mix

dry ice (optional)

1. Fill a cocktail shaker with ice.

2. Add all the ingredients for the alcoholic or nonalcoholic version, depending on your preference.

3. Shake well until chilled.

4. Strain the mixture into a chilled martini glass.

5. Add a small piece of dry ice to the glass, if desired, taking care to handle the dry ice with gloves or tongs to avoid injury.

WORD TO THE WOEFUL

As delightfully dreadful as dry ice can be, it can also be dangerous. While the danger can be intoxicating, we recommend taking care. Always use protective gloves when handling dry ice and never touch it with bare hands. It can cause skin burns. Dry ice should never be consumed, as it can cause severe injury or harm.

CLUB-HORNED GRASSHOPPER

These unique insects thrive in the forest surrounding Nevermore Academy, and are often excellent garnishes for a potion or two. In honor of these little creatures, try this minty sweet treat. Refreshing, and with fewer legs to get stuck in your teeth.

Yield: 1 drink | Prep time: 5 minutes

1 ounce green crème de menthe or green crème de menthe syrup (for nonalcoholic version)

1 ounce white crème de cacao or white chocolate syrup (for nonalcoholic version)

1 ounce heavy cream

fresh mint sprigs, for garnish

1. In a cocktail shaker filled with ice, combine the crème de menthe, crème de cacao, and heavy cream for the alcoholic version or the syrups and heavy cream for the nonalcoholic version.

2. Shake vigorously until well combined and chilled.

3. Strain the mixture into a chilled martini glass.

4. Garnish with fresh mint sprigs and serve immediately.

CORPSE REVIVER

Have you been practicing your necromancy? It's a difficult spell, and requires a lot of concentration. To relax after a long day of casting, brew up this cocktail. Want to invite the entire coven? You can make this cocktail in a large batch by scaling up the recipe and mixing all the ingredients in a cauldron—or a pitcher. Be sure to add ice when serving.

Yield: 1 drink | Prep time: 5 minutes

¾ ounce gin
¾ ounce Cointreau
¾ ounce Lillet Blanc
¾ ounce fresh lemon juice
1 dash absinthe
lemon twist, for garnish

1. Fill a cocktail shaker with ice.

2. Add the gin, Cointreau, Lillet Blanc, and fresh lemon juice to the shaker.

3. Add a dash of absinthe to the shaker (if you don't have absinthe, you can use another anise-flavored liqueur like Pernod).

4. Shake well until chilled.

5. Strain the cocktail into a chilled cocktail glass.

6. Garnish with a lemon twist.

POE'S CUP

Named after the intense annual boat race held every year on the river, this take on a Pimm's Cup is a refreshing beverage to sip on a hot day while you watch teenagers sabotage each other's boats. It's so nice to see the future in our vicious youths.

Yield: 1 drink | Prep time: 5 minutes

2 ounces Pimm's No. 1 (omit for nonalcoholic version)

3 ounces lemon-lime soda or ginger ale

1 ounce fresh lemon juice

1 cucumber slice

1 sliced strawberry

1 sprig fresh mint

lemon twist and additional cucumber and strawberry slices, for garnishing (optional)

1. In a tall glass filled with ice, combine Pimm's No. 1 (for alcoholic version only), lemon-lime soda or ginger ale, and fresh lemon juice.

2. Add the cucumber slice, strawberry slices, and sprig of mint to the glass.

3. Stir gently to combine.

4. Garnish with additional cucumber and strawberry slices, a lemon twist (optional), and a sprig of mint.

WORD TO THE WOEFUL

On a particularly warm day, you may require a more refreshing cocktail. In this case, muddle the cucumber, strawberry, and mint in the bottom of the glass before adding the other ingredients.

MARY SHELLEY'S MONSTROUS SANGRIA

Monsters have always been at the heart of the Addams family, and now they make up the hallowed halls of Nevermore. Who better to know monsters than one of their venerable mothers, the great Mary Shelley? Combine pieces of various fruits together to make your own creation.

Yield: 6 to 8 servings | Prep time: 10 minutes, plus 2 hours to chill

1 bottle red wine (or any fruit juice for nonalcoholic version)

¼ cup brandy (optional)

¼ cup orange liqueur, such as triple sec (optional)

¼ cup fresh orange juice

¼ cup fresh lemon juice

¼ cup sugar (or honey for a healthier option)

1 orange, sliced

1 lemon, sliced

1 apple, diced

1 cup sparkling water (or lemon-lime soda for a sweeter taste)

fresh mint leaves, for garnishing

1. In a large pitcher, combine the red wine (or fruit juice), brandy (if using), orange liqueur (if using), orange juice, lemon juice, and sugar. Stir until the sugar is dissolved.

2. Add the sliced orange, sliced lemon, and diced apple to the pitcher and stir.

3. Chill the mixture in the refrigerator for at least 2 hours or overnight to let the flavors meld together.

4. Just before serving, add the sparkling water (or lemon-lime soda) to the pitcher and stir.

5. Serve the sangria over ice cubes in individual glasses.

6. Garnish with fresh mint leaves.

WORD TO THE WOEFUL
Don't you love red wine? The bloody color is so welcoming. Feel the freedom to use any type of red wine that you like, such as merlot, cabernet sauvignon, or pinot noir.

CONVERSIONS

Volume

U.S.	U.S. Equivalent	Metric
1 tablespoon (3 teaspoons)	½ fluid ounce	15 milliliters
¼ cup	2 fluid ounces	60 milliliters
⅓ cup	3 fluid ounces	90 milliliters
½ cup	4 fluid ounces	120 milliliters
⅔ cup	5 fluid ounces	150 milliliters
¾ cup	6 fluid ounces	180 milliliters
1 cup	8 fluid ounces	240 milliliters
2 cups	16 fluid ounces	480 milliliters

Weight

U.S.	Metric
½ ounce	15 grams
1 ounce	30 grams
2 ounces	60 grams
¼ pound	115 grams
⅓ pound	150 grams
½ pound	225 grams
¾ pound	350 grams
1 pound	450 grams

Temperature

Fahrenheit (°F)	Celsius (°C)	Fahrenheit (°F)	Celsius (°C)
70°F	20°C	220°F	105°C
100°F	40°C	240°F	115°C
120°F	50°C	260°F	125°C
130°F	55°C	280°F	140°C
140°F	60°C	300°F	150°C
150°F	65°C	325°F	165°C
160°F	70°C	350°F	175°C
170°F	75°C	375°F	190°C
180°F	80°C	400°F	200°C
190°F	90°C	425°F	220°C
200°F	95°C	450°F	230°C